THE RATCHET

A COOL LOOK AT THE EUROPEAN UNION

PART I
THE MAELSTRO[

PART II
DEFEATISM OR RESURGENCE? 1999

by

John Rennie Stewardson

The June Press

"My congratulations on an elegantly written and thoroughly researched book... You have brought a mine of information to this subject and a well thought-out structured analysis. This deserves a wider circulation... This comprehensive analysis ... excellent work"
Bill Jamieson, former Economics Editor, Sunday Telegraph now Executive Editor, The Scotsman

"I found it most informative"
City Editor, The Daily Telegraph

"...it is an excellent publication"
Lord Rees-Mogg, former Editor of The Times

"I found it a most interesting analysis of an often misunderstood area of concern"
Editorial Director, Faber and Faber

"I read it with the greatest interest and with which I found myself in almost entire agreement"
Lord Howell of Guildford, Member of the House of Lords Select Committee on the European Communities

"I like it and agree with much of it"
Professor Patrick Minford, Professor of Economics at Cardiff Business School

"Very interesting ... very useful document"
Ruth Lea, Head of Policy, Institute of Directors

"May I congratulate you on the excellent research"
Sir Archibold Hamilton MP, Chairman 1922 Committee

First published in Great Britain in 2000

By the June Press Limited
PO Box 9984, London W12 8WZ
Tel and Fax: 020-8746 1206
Email: info@junepress.com
Web Site: www.junepress.com

ISBN 0-9534697-1- 9

Book design by Alice Leach

Printed by Printcentre Wales

THE AUTHOR

John Rennie Stewardson was at Charterhouse and then studied law and modern languages at St. Johns College, Cambridge. He was a Lieutenant in the RNVR and was active in the Battle of the Atlantic 1942-46.

A barrister, and solicitor in private practise until becoming Corporate Legal Adviser with Imperial Tobacco Plc, Company Secretary of Consolidated Gold Field Plc and Secretary of the Advertising Association. The Advertising Association is a confederation of associations representing television and radio, newspapers, magazines and all forms of marketing and advertising.

Throughout the 1980s he was regularly involved in the Brussels-Strasbourg-Westminster-Whitehall arena.

PREFACE

I wrote "**The Maelstrom**" in the Spring of 1997, and circulated it principally to Government and Opposition leaders in both Houses of Parliament, civil servants, newspaper and magazine editors and journalists, writers and academics. Two and a half years on, I have written "**Defeatism or Resurgence?**", commenting on that interim period which included the signing of the Amsterdam Treaty in October 1997, and musing over what may eventuate in the EU and what positions and courses might be adopted by the UK. I now introduce these two Papers together under the overall title of "**The Ratchet - A Cool Look at the European Union**", and I will refer to them as Part I and Part II. They are the observations of a concerned English Europe-watcher whose credentials I give in the Introduction to Part I.

In **Part I** I started with a brief outline of the historical reasons underlying why and how this enormous political enterprise was undertaken. I then touched on some of the reasons for the discord amongst the Member States, sometimes raging, sometimes quiescent, but ever-present like an undulant fever. Next I discussed the various institutions of the European Union (EU): the overbearing power and intrusiveness of the European Commission (the Commission), its ongoing legislative outpourings and its ambitions to being the Executive government; the European Court of Justice (ECJ) and its character as an administrative agency enforcing the Treaties, quite unlike a Court as understood in Britain and predominant over the Courts of all Member States; the Council of Ministers, in theory the democratic element in the whole EU structure, but an element often more apparent than real; the European Parliament (EP), dominated by the Socialist-Communist parties, with no law-making powers, but the ability to reject or amend certain forms of legislation and an increasing ambit of authority; the Court of Auditors, with its oversight of EU budgetary revenue and expenditure, but with no powers of enforcement or correction. I also considered the characteristic secretiveness of the EU, its disastrous Common Agricultural Policy (CAP) and Common Fisheries Policy (CFP), and its inexorable thrust towards federal union. I then went on to consider a number of changes to the structure and operation of the EU which should be accomplished if it were to be suitable for continued membership by the UK. I moved on to envisage the shape of things to come if the UK remained a Member without the necessary changes being achieved. And finally I outlined the encouraging scenario open to the UK in the event of its rediscovering the self-belief, courage and determination to leave the EU and advance again in its historic independence freed from the dead-weight of bureaucratic, socialist structures and dogma.

In **Part II**, in considering the period from May 1997 onward and into the future, I start with a brief tour d'horizon and then comment on:

- the continual progressive shift, past and present, towards an integrated federal union and the ever more open declaration of that objective by many leaders in Member States other than the UK;
- the Amsterdam Treaty and its precursors, and the widening and deepening of the powers of the Commission and the EP as an ongoing process towards the ever-maintained goal of federal union;
- the single currency adopted by 11 Member States and the contortions and fudging necessary for several of them to comply with the Maastricht convergence criteria; the euro's performance; the Economic and Monetary Union (EMU); and the European Central Bank (ECB) and the fierce in-fighting over the appointment of its President;
- the conduct of the Commission and its involvement in corruption and fraud;
- the EP, its widening powers and its part in the resignation of the Commissioners;

- the EU Budget, the UK rebate and the unachieved amendment of CAP;
- the question of Enlargement: the EU and NATO;
- some developments in the UK with relevance to the EU;
- the Labour Government's acceptance of the Social Chapter and the minimum wages and working hours regulations and its obvious drive towards the single currency and ever more integration with the EU;
- the policies and attitudes of UK Governments regarding the Community;
- and where to go from here?

At the end of Part II I have put a Further List of Reading and Reference, and of course the list in Part I remains as interesting as ever.

PART I

THE MAELSTROM

I think our country sinks beneath the yoke; it weeps, it bleeds:
and each new day a gash is added to her wounds
Macbeth, Act IV, Scene 3

PART I

THE MAELSTROM

CONTENTS

INTRODUCTION

In the country of the blind, the one-eyed man is king. As a Europe-watcher I would like to put forward my perceptions and impressions of the **European Community**. You may ask why should you listen to me, how am I one of the relatively few "one-eyed". I would reply that I was a lawyer in big companies who throughout the 1980s lobbied in Brussels and Strasbourg, Whitehall and Westminster on behalf of a significant Trade Association. This work involved regularly attending Parliamentary Sessions in Strasbourg; meeting MEPs there and in London; meetings at various stages with the drafters of Directives in Brussels; meetings in Whitehall with the Home Office and Department of Trade civil servants who negotiate the Draft Directives in Brussels; holding briefing sessions for MPs and Peers in Westminster, and so on. I also drafted for my Trade Association various memoranda for the House of Lords Select Committee on the European Communities and for the House of Commons Home Affairs Committee on Transfrontier Broadcasting, and with colleagues gave oral evidence to both those Committees. As a background to this work, I have of course used the Treaty of Rome, the Single European Act, the Maastricht Treaty, and the Draft Constitution (which is intended progressively to replace the Treaties), and I have at various times ploughed through their lengthy, turgid and alien provisions until my wits were numbed. In addition, I have no political or commercial axe to grind, but as an Englishman with a deep interest in the continuing good of my country, I say it as I see it. So I invite you to give me a hearing, which I hope may add something to your own European perspective. Will you please bear in mind that where I refer to fear, dislike or criticism between countries, I am referring to attitudes between Governments, or towards individuals in their public capacity, or am making generalizations about peoples. Man is good, bad or average the world over, and man-to-man assessments are made on a human, rather than a political, basis.

Increasingly during one's encounter with this vital subject, the inward eye discerns that the European Community is part Alice in Wonderland and part "1984" and Animal Farm — schizophrenic and destructive — and we are in its vortex. I think "vortex" is apt, meaning, "a way of life or situation that engulfs one irresistibly or remorselessly, taking up all one's attention or energies".

Chapter One

BUT WHAT IS IT ALL FOR?

This is a question not often enough asked nowadays in the welter of the day-to-day struggle with the Community's institutions. The original stimulus was the pervasive fear across Western Europe in the late 1940s that Germany might later once again become the military aggressor. France had been invaded three times in seventy years, and she as well as Belgium, Holland, Luxembourg, Denmark and Norway had all been humiliated and occupied by the brutal German war machine. In addition, Italy, Greece, Austria and Finland as well as the Eastern European countries had all been devastated in the same holocaust. Ireland, Spain, Portugal and Sweden had been in varying degrees of neutrality. Only the United Kingdom was on the victorious side, although financially ruined in the process. Desperate situations may need desperate measures, but the structure created to safeguard Europe's future bore the seeds of its own failure. Now, forty years on, a poll taken in mid-January 1999 amongst the four biggest Member States, the UK, Germany, France and Italy, by a clear consensus shows the expectation that Germany has or will become the dominant power in the Community, and that this outcome is "disliked" (the bland word used to conceal more deep-set emotions) — a blinding flash of the obvious, one might say.

This Byzantine sprawl of institutions housed in over 200 buildings in Brussels, Luxembourg and Strasbourg, with its 24 Directorates-General, its 700 Committees, its rain-forests' worth of paper and its financial cost in the hundreds of billions has created a dirigiste bureaucracy constantly causing tension and frustration. These feelings are not only between Member States, but also within each and every Member State as their respective Governments seek to implement some aspect of the Community's programme. So by a terrible irony the frightened creators of this monster set in motion a course of events which is inexorably leading to the very situation that they were bent on avoiding.

How did the Community come to be cast in the mould of a bureaucratic oligarchy? The UK did not participate in the Messina Conference in 1955 held between the original Six, Germany, France, Italy, Netherlands, Belgium and Luxembourg. With hindsight this was a crucial misjudgment, because we missed the vital opportunity of taking a leading role in shaping the institutions and the main thrust of the Treaty of Rome. But in the mid-1950s UK Government thinking was still on the lines of Empire, Commonwealth and the US special relationship, and the UK lacked the fear-driven imperative of the five of the Six all of which had suffered so much through Nazi conquest. The greatest and most fatal flaw in the foundation of the Community was giving the European Commission the power of **initiate** legislation.

One can imagine that such a decision was less at odds with continental bureaucratic socialism than with the British form of governance, and presumably the UK would have vetoed the proposal had it attended the Messina Conference. Nevertheless it is extraordinary that a group of nations should all abdicate their foremost power of government — initiating laws and regulations — and cede that power to a new, unelected, unrepresentative civil service. Civil servants normally **serve** Governments. As far as I am aware, this abnormal yielding of power in the European Community is without parallel anywhere else in the world.

The UK having set its face against the Messina Conference, the Treaty of Rome came into effect in 1957 without the UK being a signatory (a "High Contracting Party", in the jargon). UK Governmental attitudes gradually changed and negotiations for us to join the Community were carried out in 1961 and 1967, and each time our membership was vetoed by France. Its President, de Gaulle, a junior general who never fought any military operations, had fled to England on France's collapse in May 1940, and there rallied the Free French forces. Always prickly, he bitterly resented having to be totally dependent on the British. We will never know the true weight given by him to this resentment when he turned down our approaches in 1961 and 1967.

In 1970 the UK Government under Edward Heath made further overtures to the Community for membership. After de Gaulle's departure, the Community's attitude modified to the extent that if entry terms were sufficiently burdensome for the UK and beneficial to the other Members, we could join. Rapidly and just in time before we signed the Accession to the Treaty, the Community introduced the Common Fisheries Policy, whereby our rich fishing waters were made a "common resource". In addition, our contribution to the Community budget funds was disproportionately high, making us the second biggest contributor. So Heath took us in to the Community at the wrong time and on the wrong terms.

If only the process had stopped after the 1957 Treaty of Rome, there would have been a hope of harmony in creating better and simpler trade conditions, but that alone would not have met the secret federal ambitions widespread among the other Member States. The next progression was the Single European Act of 1986. This took a significant leap forward towards the federal goal by surrendering the veto in various contexts. The veto is the mechanism whereby the UK can have some control over developments in the Community, and whenever it is replaced by qualified majority voting (QMV), the UK's often friendless position in meetings of the Council of Ministers is rendered impotent. It is difficult to understand Mrs. Thatcher's acceptance of the Single European Act, having regard to her subsequent strong Bruges speech and her distrust of her old adversary Jacques Delors, the then President of the European Commission. I believe that the Foreign Office, which is pro-Europe (at any price?) and has an inglorious record in fighting the UK corner, in its briefing of her advocated the Act as forwarding the trade objectives and ignored or played down the pro-federal implications of the removal of the veto in several further areas. However, this does not exonerate Mrs. Thatcher, who could not have sought a sufficient spectrum of advice.

There were wise counsels who went unheeded, particularly Enoch Powell and Lord Denning. The latter, one of our greatest jurists, warned in the House of Lords debate on the fateful European Communities (Amendment) Bill that it involved not only economic union but also political and legal unity, that our sovereignty would be seriously eroded, and that the aim was to transform Europe into a single nation, with Westminster as a subordinate body.

Maastricht produced the Consolidated Treaty on European Union, which incorporated the Maastricht developments into the Treaty of Rome as amended by the Single European Act. Maastricht was yet a further big step towards the federal goal, with qualified majority voting (QMV) on many more subjects, and whole new fields opened up for Community intrusion, and it paves the way towards Economic and Monetary Union (EMU) and the single currency.

Chapter Two

WHY SO MUCH DISCORD?

Each of the now 15 Member States is totally distinct from all the others on every count one can think of: history; maturity as a nation; experience on the world stage; geography; climate; religion; language; population; size; politics; legal system; industry; technological advance; military strength; relative wealth or poverty; temperament; traditions; habits; mores; culture; strategic objectives. I have laboured the differences to highlight the supreme folly of struggling onward towards Federal Union.

And in some ways, the UK is even more distinct from the mainland European countries. We are an island nation, independent for nearly a thousand years, having withstood threatened invasion from the Spanish Armada, Napoleon and Hitler. A hundred years and more ago we were the rulers of the world's greatest Empire, at a time when some of Europe's countries were still adjusting to new nationhood. Bismarck united various provinces to create Germany and similarly Garibaldi unified Italy, both in the 1870s. Belgium became independent in the 1830s. The Kingdom of the Netherlands came into existence after Waterloo in 1815. Modern Greece became independent at the end of the 1820s. Ireland became a republic in 1922. The tiny principality of Luxembourg became a separate grand duchy in 1890, upon the death of the King of the Netherlands, its previous owner. In more recent times, say, over the last 50 years, and judging by such criteria as membership of the UN Security Council, membership of the G7 group of industrial nations, nuclear capability, world trade, world financial markets, and links with Commonwealth and the Pacific rim, there are really only three major Member States of the Community — the UK, Germany and France. And yet Germany-France is the EC axis, and the UK is the Member State the most often at odds with the others, frequently forming a minority of one. The reasons for this are various, largely stemming from our very different-ness. We were the only nation in Europe (with the massive alliance of the USA and our Empire and Commonwealth contingents) to win the Second World War, in which Germany, Austria and Italy were defeated, and France, Belgium, the Netherlands, Luxembourg, Denmark and Greece were liberated by us and our allies from the horrors of Nazi occupation. Gratitude is an emotion experienced between individuals rather than nations, but it is ironic that particularly of more recent times a prominent attitude in the Community is anti-Anglo-Saxon, or more specifically, anti-Anglo-American. This attitude varies from country to country and springs from sources such as guilt and shame for its past actions, failures or inaction, envy, satisfaction at our much lowlier standing since loss of Empire. "How are the mighty fallen" always tends to give some satisfaction to others.

But all is far from sweetness and light amongst the rest of the Community. The majority fear and dislike Germany, and with good cause. France, still haunted by her military and moral collapse in 1940, manages to look *de haut en bas* on everyone, especially the Belgians and the Spanish; in the latter case, one assumes this is not on ethnic grounds, because the Moors invaded and settled large parts of France for centuries, up as far as Poitiers. The Northern Members tend to scorn, sometimes openly, the Southern Members, and more particularly the poor Members Spain, Portugal, Greece and Ireland. The Dutch cannot stand the Germans. Belgium is almost two countries, with Walloon and Fleming vehemently hostile to each other. Italy has its Lombard League wanting separation from the South, and its recent Prime Minister and some 200 Parliamentarians have been subject to criminal charges. Tiny Luxembourg has to fall into line with Belgium, and by extension with Germany.

The rest of the Community seem to like ambushing us in Council of Ministers' meetings and generally opposing us, and they relish our discomfiture, not only because of the attitudes referred to above, but also because we obstruct or resist many things being initiated. And we do resist many trends and initiatives, because they are ill-founded and wrong, and stem from a fundamentally flawed structure and interventionist mentality.

Chapter Three

THE ANATOMY OF THE MONSTER

They bring smooth comforts false, Worse than true wrongs
Henry IV, Part II, Induction

If Comrade Napoleon says it, it must be right
Animal Farm

The concept of the structure flows from the political orientation of the majority of Community Members which is primarily bureaucratic socialism. Even making allowances for that, it is still extraordinary that any group of countries should set up as its centrepiece a monolithic civil service, **the European Commission**, and endow it with the power and duty of **initiating**, overseeing and enforcing legislation. — (Articles 155-163). I cannot think of any democracy in the world where this system exists or would be allowed to exist, and it would be complete anathema to any one-party government or dictatorship. As it is, the Commission increasingly pries into every nook and cranny of every Member State's existence, and produces restrictive and damaging regulations. This is done in contemptuous disregard of the "subsidiarity" rule (Treaty, Article 3b) which provides that the Commission shall regulate only when it cannot be done effectively by the Member State. There are hundreds of examples of this disastrous over-regulation recorded in *The Mad Officials* and *The Castle of Lies*, both by Booker and North. Some examples are bizarre, some are farcical, many show a lack of plain common sense on the part of the Commission, all result in individuals and businesses suffering significant losses or going to the wall. It is incredible that Member States put up with it. But then, what actually happens is that many

Member States tacitly accept the regulations, and then ignore or fail to implement them. We, on the other hand, suffer twice. We suffer opprobrium for arguing about the regulations, and once they are in force, we are punctilious in implementing them to the full. And more than to the full, for our Department of Trade and Ministry of Agriculture both have a record for going beyond the strict requirements of the rules, increasing the damage already caused. The Commission pumps out thousands of regulations — some 3,000 in 1995 — creating loss, bankruptcy, unemployment and ill-will wherever their shadow falls. In addition to initiating legislation, the Commission has wide powers of overseeing the observance of its legislation and means of enforcement (Article 155), and also it is the designated body to negotiate with foreign organisations and institutions such as GATT (superseded by the World Trade Organization) (Treaty, Articles 228 and 229) — another example of how infinitely more powerful it is than any other civil service in the world. However, this situation ceases to be incredible when it is realised that according to the secret agenda, rapidly becoming less secret, the President of the Commission Jacques Santer and his Commissioners are in effect to be the Chief Executive and Board of Directors of the Federal Union of Europe Plc.

The so-called judicial system supporting the Commission is the **European Court of Justice** (Articles 164-188) which sits in Luxembourg. The Court is manned by a judge from each of the 15 Member States, and by several Advocates-General who in each case write an Opinion which is frequently taken as the basis of the Court's Judgement on the issue before it. In fact, only four members of the Court in 1995/6 were judges or qualified to be judges in their own country. The Court is not a Court as we in England understand it; it is more in the nature of an administrative agency enforcing the Treaties, or more particularly what the Court thinks the Treaties could and should mean.

The position is made intolerably worse by two critical factors:

first, there is no appeal system, so the ECJ is the ultimate arbiter; and second, the Court prevails over our highest national Courts in all matters. So a case in England can go right up through the High Court, the Court of Appeal and the House of Lords, and then be reversed by the ECJ with its unsatisfactory system and panel of judges.

The English legal system is the basis of the legal systems throughout the USA and the various Commonwealth countries around the world, and it is totally different from the systems of all the other Member States of the Community, which are based on Roman law. This is yet another difference between us and the rest of the Community. So it is not difficult to see that the English judge can carry little or no weight on this Tribunal.

The Council of Ministers (Articles 145-154) is in theory the democratic element in the Community. It meets at various times and places during the year, and each Member State is represented by the relevant Government Minister according to the business in hand, be it Agriculture, Finance, Trade or otherwise. So there is the element of Government oversight; but in reality some 80% of the decisions are agreed beforehand between the Commission and the Committee of Permanent Representatives of the Member States (COREPER) so that at the Council of Ministers meetings, the Ministers are largely rubber-stamping what has already been agreed.

A serious drawback to the Council of Ministers is its disproportionate voting basis which is on a scale from 10 to 2, between biggest and smallest Member States, which greatly favours the latter. The UK has 10 votes and tiny Luxembourg, with a population smaller than Bristol or Leeds, has 2 votes. If the voting were based on **population**, Luxembourg would have 1 vote and the UK 155 votes. This system of voting laid down in the Treaty (Article 148) should be changed.

The Community **Parliament**, that Diet of Make-believe, (Articles 137-144) started life as an unelected Assembly, but has been an elected body since 1979, although it is still largely a talking-shop. Its powers have been widened, and there is the wish in some European quarters to extend them further. But I think it will always be an ineffectual body, if for no other reason than because the Community is moving towards more and more power for the Commission and its President, so that when (not if) the Community becomes a Federal Union, the President and Commission will form the operative authority. The Parliament is dominated by the Socialist-Communist groups, which may suit the UK Labour Party, but the UK Conservative MEPs have very little voice and are affiliated to their nearest allies who are the European Peoples Party (EPP) which is pro-federalist. In any event, the 81 UK MEPs each cover wide areas of the home country and for the most part are shadowy figures hardly known in their constituencies, and can do very little. How many people actually know the name and face of their MEP?

One of the many absurdities and shortcomings of the Community is the arrangement for Parliament Sessions. These occur for one week every month usually ten times a year, and for each of those weeks hundreds of Commission officials, hundreds of MEPs, and thousands of big grey tin cabin trunks full of papers form a gigantic migration from Brussels and all over Europe to Strasbourg. Then at the end of each of those weeks, the huge convoy makes its way back to Brussels and elsewhere, until the next time. This is because the Member States, ever fighting their national corner, cannot agree upon a commercially sensible disposition of the institutions of the Community. This means that those institutions are spread over some 200 buildings in Brussels, Strasbourg and Luxembourg, thus involving duplication and waste of money and of time shuttling between the three main centres. It was recently proposed by a supporter of one of the Welsh or Scottish political parties that the House of Commons should go "on circuit", sitting regularly in turn in London, Cardiff and Edinburgh, with of course the attendant battalions of MPs, civil servants, assistants and tin boxes. This would be ludicrous and hugely wasteful, just as it is in the Community, and puts the Community's folly, inefficiency and wastefulness into clearer perspective.

Yet another disadvantage of the system, the magnitude of which is only grasped when it is thought through, is the problem of **interpreting** in sessions of Parliament and Committees, and **translating**. These are two quite distinct functions: interpreting is instantaneous into headphones during meetings; translating is translation of the written word, after meetings, for circulation in each of the languages of the 15 Member States. It is not easy to find interpreters and translators of sufficiently high calibre, and I have known meetings postponed for lack of interpreters, and I have also listened to interpreters of widely differing standards of efficiency. It is also not hard to imagine differences and misunderstandings arising due to divergences and nuances of meaning. At the end of each day's proceedings, teams of translators labour to produce and have printed an accurate record in all the languages of the Community, for circulation the following day. The recorded version for each Member State is identified by a different-coloured front page. The whole problem of interpreting and translating will become ever more complex and acute as the Community further enlarges.

The Treaty (Article 188a-c) provides for a **Court of Auditors** to check that all Community revenue has been received, all expenditure incurred lawfully, and whether financial management has been sound. This is a necessary and useful institution, but unfortunately it has been given no powers of enforcement, so it is not allowed to be as effective as it should be. The Court of Auditors' conservative estimate has highlighted an annual loss of £5-6 billion through fraud amongst Member States, but little or nothing has been done about it. The giving of effective investigation and enforcement powers to the Court of Auditors is one of the essential changes in Community institutions that the UK should fight for. Fraud and corruption are widespread in the Community to the tune of billions, and are largely unchecked and unpunished. Member

States claim subsidies for greater quantities than actually exist, or sometimes for non-existent quantities, of rape seed oil, or tobacco or milk, and so on. Other claims are made for multiple "export" subsidies, when those concerned are merely transporting cereals or dairy products round from one Member State to another. Individual Member States are not keen to Report their nationals' frauds, because then that particular Member State bears the cost, whereas if the fraud is unreported, the loss is borne by the Community as a whole. Also, large sums of money paid to poor Member States and regions under the Structural Funds and Cohesion Fund (Treaty, Article 130a-e and Protocol) are misappropriated and unaccounted for. Little or no effort is made to deal with these defalcations. A Report produced for the Commission by the top international accountants Deloitte & Touche, and commented upon in the press (24 April 1997), found that international fraud is costing Community countries up to £45 billion a year, and the problem is growing.

Looking further at **the characteristics of the Community**, there is the flawed nature of the structure and institutions already touched on. It is becoming an increasingly centralized authoritarian bureaucracy in its inexorable shift to a Federal Union, by which stage it will be near-totalitarian. Whether this stage will be reached while the Presidency of the Commission is held by Jacques Santer, that unblushful schizophrene with delusions of adequacy, is not known. In the Community everything is compromise, which leaves all parties dissatisfied. Regarding the Presidency of the Commission, it is absurd that that increasingly important post is filled by someone from Luxembourg, a tiny Grand Duchy with no experience or standing in the international scene. On the other hand, from whichever Member State a person is appointed, the remaining Member States will be dissatisfied, no doubt for varying reasons.

This comes back to the standpoint that it is highly undesirable, and potentially dangerous, that the Commission and its President should have so much power. The movement to increasing this power should be stopped and reversed, so that the Commission ceases to be the engine of the Community, and takes up a traditional civil service role.

> *When I use a word, it means just what I choose it to mean*
> *- neither more nor less*
> Alice Through the Looking Glass

Leaving aside the all-pervading regulatory intrusiveness of the Commission into all aspects of national life, and the cumbersome procedures provided by the Treaty (for example, Article 189b and c and the so-called negative assent procedure regarding the adoption of legislation), the **drafting** of legislation by the Commission officials is constantly the cause of misunderstanding, and doubt or divergence in interpretation. By the standards of English Parliamentary draftsmanship, the Treaty is long-winded, tortuous, imprecise, often ambiguous, and sometimes so loosely or widely drawn as to give huge latitude for "compliance", for example, Article 104c, 2(a) and (b) and the Protocol on the excessive deficit procedure, laying down criteria for government debt and budgetary deficit. This Article (together with Article 109j and the Protocol) forms the acid test for admission to the single currency, and yet it contains words and phrases of such elasticity as to permit the Commission endless scope for accepting fudge after fudge. And as the statistical data concerning Convergence is to be provided by the Commission (Convergence Protocol, Article 5), the **political** nature of the whole enterprise is again revealed to all who wish to see.

Other **weasel words and phrases** include:-

- "ever closer union" (Preamble and Article A) now claimed to have always meant federal union, but in the 1957 Treaty of Rome it seemed to refer to "unity of their economies".

- "acquis communautaire" (Article B) which I mention later.

- "single institutional framework" (Article C) does this refer to a Constitution for the Federal Union?

- "general political guidelines" (Article D) this catch-all phrase relates to the development of the Community and clearly implies the impetus towards federalism.

- "by common accord" appears at various places in the Treaty; it seems distinct from unanimity and from a qualified majority.

- "subsidiarity" (Article 3b) although in the Treaty, it is believed to be unenforceable as too vague and it was described as "gobbledegook" by Lord Mackenzie Stuart, the former British President of the Court of Justice.

However, aside from the very different drafting style of the continental bureaucrat, much of the labyrinthine obscurity and ambiguity may be a conscious device to give the Commission endless scope to act as it wishes under the aegis of the Treaty.

Another unattractive characteristic of the Commission is its **secretiveness**. This is due partly to the arrogance of a dirigiste bureaucracy, but also to the wish to keep its ultimate goal of Federal Union camouflaged for as long as possible. It has never been easy to get early drafts of Directives, for the purpose of conferring with Ministries or lobbying. After Maastricht, it was impossible for quite a time to get a copy of the amended Treaty, either from Brussels or from HM Stationery Office. This shameful public service failure was rectified by a praiseworthy private enterprise on the part of the British Management Data Foundation (Director, Brigadier Anthony Cowgill) who published a very useful and excellent copy with explanatory preface. It is scandalous that the Commission and HM Government should keep the voting public in the dark about the most momentous series of events of this century (the two World Wars aside). Brussels officials maintain that Council of Ministers meetings are secret and papers concerning these are not available. Indeed, representatives of the Council of Ministers in a court case in the ECJ stated that "there is no principle of Community law which gives citizens the right to EU documents". Likewise, when papers for meetings are prepared by the Commission, they are supplied by electronic mail to Bonn and Paris, but for London they are frequently consigned to the Belgian postal service which takes up to ten days. This can mean that the UK is ill-prepared for the meeting in question.

The Community has from the beginning been built up in **secrecy**, and Claude Cheysson, former French Foreign Minister and Commissioner in an interview (*Le Figaro*, 7th May 1994) proclaimed that it could only have been done in the absence of democracy. Another example of secrecy concerns the draft **Constitution** of the European Union. Post-Maastricht, in 1993 the Committee on Institutional Affairs of the European Parliament produced a Draft Report and a working document which were not readily available from officials or from Government. But fortunately another private source, the Campaign Against Euro-Federalism, made the texts available. The draft Constitution is federal, giving effect to the long-term goal of political union, reinforcing the Commission's powers, and "putting an end to the fiction of the abiding intact sovereignty of the Member States". The Constitution would progressively replace the Treaties, and would provide for Member States deciding to **leave** the Union to have specific Agreements granting them "preferential associate status". I have not seen any later Draft of this Constitution, which I guess very few people have heard of, but I expect that substantial progress is being made somewhere behind closed doors.

Stuffing the ears of men with false reports
Henry IV, Part II, Induction

How far the Commission's secrecy over the decades, particularly about its federal goal, has misled the UK Government is difficult to guess. How far has the latter been a dupe, and how far a fellow conspirator? Maybe it half understood the federal agenda, but thought it would not happen, and therefore it was safe to ignore it. Our Government has always grossly underestimated the momentum of the intense and unswerving drive of the Community eventually to be federal, and this failure of grasp must largely be the fault of the Foreign Office. It too, having lost an Empire, has not really found a role. How far did it mislead Edward Heath in 1970-2? Having said in his White Paper of 1971 (Command 4715), that there was "no question of any erosion of essential national sovereignty", Heath now claims that he knew all along that sovereignty would be surrendered. Indeed, Heath told Parliament that "we should frankly recognise this surrender of sovereignty and its purpose" (Hansard, 17th November 1966). His statement in his 1971 White Paper was therefore a cynical and shameful deception of the British people and an abuse of democracy. This dishonesty followed the political approach suggested by Peter (later Lord) Thorneycroft in his pamphlet *Design for Europe* published in June 1947. In it, regarding entry into the European Union, he said: "... no Government dependent upon a democratic vote could possibly agree in advance to the sacrifices any adequate plan must involve. The people must be led slowly and unconsciously into the abandonment of their traditional economic defences". The people have been led by the nose ever since, "**slowly and unconsciously**" along this fateful trail. Edmund Burke was right in saying that "the people never give up their liberty but under some delusion". And the Foreign Office, following its traditional agenda, surely misled Mrs. Thatcher in 1986 about the significance of the Single European Act.

But the attitude towards the federal goal has become more open on the continent in only the last 5 years or so. Throughout the 1980s whenever working in Brussels, Strasbourg or Luxembourg, I never heard mention of the federal agenda. Indeed, only in the mid-1980s was the change from EEC to EC noticeable — the middle symbol standing for "Economic" was dropped, to make way for the "European Community".

Here in the UK our Governments, present and past, have been sleep-walking in the Community, and even now continue to do so. The mantra of "being at the heart of Europe" is repeated by Ministers as if under hypnosis. They deny that there is an inexorable drive towards federal union and that the drive is gathering momentum amongst all the other 14 Member States.

This denial is in the face of daily repetition of those facts by numbers of leading politicians, civil servants and bankers from the capitals and main cities around Europe. Imitating Nero in burning Rome, the Government says "wait and see", and Kenneth Clarke, that Euro-tunnel-visioned President of the Flat Earth Society, says that the countless concerns about federal union are "paranoid nonsense".

Regarding appointments by each Member State to the Commission and its Secretariat, I cannot speak from personal experience of the British contingent, because the several officials in the Directorates-General that I used to deal with were mainly Germans, Dutch or Italians. As a generalization, I believe that British officials appointed to Brussels tend to "go native" and develop the single vision of the classic EC man. This may mean that they take more seriously than their continental confrères the Commission oath of complete independence in the general interest of the Community. Be that as it may, the officials of other Member States, the French probably more than any, seemed more like hand-picked shock troops mopping up on behalf of their homeland. The French énarque élite are past-masters in the administrative pursuit of national interest. Yves-Thibault de Silguy, the French Commissioner for monetary affairs is reported as being nicknamed "Monsieur Fax" because of his apparent refusal to do anything until he receives a fax of approval from Paris. So much for the Commission oath to remain totally independent and not to seek or receive instructions from his home Government.

Another mechanism of the Community regularly referred to and used by the Commission is the **"acquis communautaire"**, broadly meaning "acquired Community practice and powers". The principle is that whenever the Community gains a certain stage or objective, that becomes an established part of the acquis communautaire and is irreversible and irretrievable. I am not aware of a provision in any of the Treaties actually creating and granting this power to the Community, but there is a passage (Treaty, Title I, Article B) which merely **assumes** its existence, and states the objective "to maintain in full the acquis communautaire and build on it ...".

Turning to one or two of the Community's most outrageous policies, the **Common Agricultural Policy** (CAP) continues to be a huge financial burden. CAP "protective" prices were first imposed in 1973, the year the UK joined the Community, and throughout the 1980s Community food prices were on average **70% higher** than world market prices. The National Consumer Council estimated in September 1995 that CAP costs an average UK family an extra £20 per week in food bills. This great lumbering mechanism, with high costs, overproduction, and fraudulent activity, is largely to feather-bed the inefficient farming industry in France and Germany. France's inefficient farming is made worse by its inheritance laws whereby property has to be inherited equally between all beneficiaries, so the size of farms becomes smaller and smaller and less economic. We all know of the butter mountains and wine lakes and the huge waste, and distortion of markets; and the absurdity of "set aside" whereby farmers are paid large sums not to grow certain crops, and at the same time they may also grow and sell a different, non-qualifying crop, thus getting two payments in respect of the same land.

A more topical aggravation is the **Common Fisheries Policy** (CFP). It is worth recalling the origins of this Policy which are perhaps now forgotten. There was nothing about Fisheries in the Treaty of Rome, so when the UK was making its further approach for membership in mid-1970, the then six members of the Community rushed through **Council Regulation 2141/70** permitting equal access for all Member States to each other's fishing waters. This Regulation was adopted immediately before the UK application was lodged, and had very dubious, if any, legitimacy under the Treaty of Rome.

The CFP is a shambles deteriorating month by month, as fish stocks diminish through over-fishing by unscrupulous foreign fleets. Measures such as restricting the number of days per month a vessel may sail merely means that that vessel owner cannot remain viable, and he will go bankrupt. When Brussels bureaucrats, unaware of fish behaviour, fix quotas for the catching of certain kinds of fish, this results in the enforced throwing back into the sea of huge quantities of "illegally" caught fish which are then dead. In 1991 the Commission's Mid-Term Review of the CFP admitted that "discards" by fishermen account for "hundreds of thousands of tons and billions of individuals" each year, 3.7 million tonnes a year according to the Food and Agriculture Organization (FAO), perhaps more than the quantities of fish actually landed.

Spain has by far the largest fishing fleet in the Community (75% of the total of all the rest put together) and are also getting a share of the UK quota by buying UK "flag boats" from bankrupted British owners. A new Spanish Armada. There is so much unpoliced fraudulent fishing, by the use of nets with too fine mesh and by catching restricted species and by using bigger and bigger vessels, that it will be very difficult to avoid this Brussels-created conservation disaster.

Whilst the CAP and the CFP are extremely damaging to our interests, even more fundamental are the related issues of the **Exchange Rate Mechanism** (ERM), **Economic and Monetary Union** (EMU) and the **Single Currency**. The Treaty states (Article 109L.4) that the conversion rates at which Member States' currencies will be fixed shall be **irrevocable**. In October 1990, members of the UK Government wanting closer European integration, mainly Howe, Hurd and Lawson, prevailed in taking the UK into the ERM at a fixed central parity of 2.95% deutschmarks to the pound, and this led to us falling into a deep recession, with rising unemployment. The Government thrashed about like a hooked fish for two years, and maintained right up to the day before we were forced out of the ERM that it was a good thing to be in. We left the ERM in October 1992, a great deal poorer, but apparently none the wiser.

This manoeuvre towards further European integration proved a disastrous blunder, and cost us very dearly. The cost of defending sterling within its ERM band, the loss of gross domestic product (GDP) in the recession, and the cost of increased unemployment have been estimated at between £68 billion and £79 billion. This ruinous débacle and much else is well covered in *There is an alternative* by Burkitt, Baimbridge & Whyman (April 1996). It seems that an ERM band is a dangerous snare, because it is fixed and may accommodate an economy at one time; but a country's economy inevitably will from time to time vary upwards or downwards, straying outside the ERM band, and then that country will be forced to wrench and distort its economy in order to regain the band. This system is the enemy of stable economy and effective governance.

The Governor of the Bank of England has said that monetary union is not essential for a Community free market, but if it is brought about, it will lead to political union. Sir Alan Walters has expressed a similar view. Sir Keith Joseph wrote in *The Times*, 26th September 1991 to the same effect. In June 1988 that arch-federalist Jacques Delors observed that an embryo European Government would emerge in the 1990s, and that 80% of all economic and social legislation would emerge from Brussels within the same time-scale. Shortly after the Bruges speech in 1988 (and Mrs. Thatcher's "No, no, no" to further integration), Martens the Belgian Prime Minister said that elimination of trade barriers would make closer political unity inevitable, leading to some form of federal European government.

The Community is in the slow track and falling behind in world markets, and is wrestling unsuccessfully with high but differing levels of unemployment and slow growth of GDP. The probability, some say certainty, is that a single currency will heighten regional inequalities and cause even greater unemployment. The UK has in effect an opt-out from the single currency (the UK Protocol in the Treaty), provided it **notifies** the Council that "it does not intend to move to the third stage" of EMU. If however the Government, Parliament and the British people by referendum decide to adopt a single currency, the UK will **no longer** "retain its powers in the field of monetary policy according to national law". We will give up those powers of control to the European Central Bank (ECB), we will pay up its subscribed capital, transfer to it our foreign reserves of £26 billion, and contribute to its reserves. The ECB will have the exclusive right to authorize the issue of bank notes within the Community (Article 105a.1.). Control of monetary policy by the ECB implicitly involves control of Government borrowing, expenditure and taxation, and would confirm our loss of effective self-government in the UK. There is already "harmonization" of VAT (Treaty, Article 99) on certain goods and services, and other areas are expected to be targeted, such as books, newspapers, public transport, food, children's clothes and house purchase. This will obviously cost untold billions. Several VAT Directives already exist and the latest Commission document is COM 328/96 which says that the present transitional system gives "Member States the illusion of having retained full sovereignty". After control of monetary policy is handed over, with conversion rates "irrevocably" fixed, and VAT and excise duties harmonized, the inevitable next step is the harmonization of income tax. After that, with our status reduced to that of a rate-capped County Council, the logical and irresistible progression will be to a Federal Union under one Constitution (a Draft of which I have already referred to), and one Government, being the Commission.

In the UK the pro-monetary union faction seems to have the support of the CBI and the BBC, both of which unquestioningly absorb and retail the Brussels propaganda. The CBI's voice should not be persuasive, because it is not what it seems. Its main spokesmen come from the large companies and are not representative of the majority. Some 97% of all UK businesses employ under 20 people; and most of them trade within a 50 mile radius of their base. Some 80% of UK companies do business only within the UK. The Federation of Small Businesses representing 70,000 firms, voted at its annual conference to **leave the Community altogether**. Again, a significant finding from one of the CBI's own surveys was that 88% of respondents were opposed to deepening integration. Even from leading UK companies the message is not consistent. The present Chairman of the giant Anglo-Dutch company Unilever is reportedly in favour of the single currency, whereas the previous Chairman, Sir Michael Perry, took a different view. When the latter gave evidence in March 1996 to the House of Lords Committee on the European Communities, he was asked what he would do if Holland were in the single currency and the UK were not. He replied that it would be a supremely irrelevant matter and he would change nothing; his Company already traditionally operated throughout the world with Governments and economies which of course vary.

Interestingly, Unilever's Annual Report & Accounts (April 1997) shows that over the previous five years its proportion of turnover and of operating profit derived from Europe has **declined**, from 57% to 49% and from 57% to 47% respectively. In the same pattern, another giant company, Shell, also Anglo-Dutch, shows in its Annual Report & Accounts (April 1997) that its earnings relating to Europe have **declined** progressively in the three years 1994-96 from 69% to 44½%. A further leading Anglo-Dutch company, Reed International shows in its Annual Report & accounts (April 1997) that only some 42% of its global market is in Europe.

Top businessmen in other leading UK companies express sceptic views about the single currency and its effect, for instance, the Chief Executives of Barclays Bank and Abbey National. Our Foreign Secretary, Malcolm Rifkind, has said the single currency would be a major step towards the end of the UK as an independent nation. In March 1997 Charles Pasqua, former French Interior Minister, chaired a seminar of politicians opposed to the single currency. The list goes on, of important voices all over Europe expressing profound misgivings.

What the blinkered bureaucrats of the Community ignore, at everyone's peril, is that the various economies are **living organisms** subject to constant or frequent change according to **market forces**. The fifteen, and later more, economies are all distinct and disparate entities, and it is the sheerest folly to subject them to the straitjacket of arbitrary fixed rates set by artificial and "guestimated" standards. This makes no **economic** sense, but then the real goal of the French-German Axis and their satellites is **political**: integration into federal union. To go forward with this crippling charade, Member States have to jump through the hoop of the **convergence** criteria (Treaty, Article 109j and its Protocol and Article 104c). Briefly, these criteria relate to (i) a government budget deficit of no more than 3% of GDP, (ii) government debt of no more than 60% of GDP, (iii) a rate of inflation within a stated formula, and (iv) long-term interest rates within certain limits. Early in 1996, analysis showed that of the 15 Member States, only tiny Luxembourg met the criteria, (which frankly, is neither here nor there). This finding was confirmed in March 1997 by Professor Wilhelm Noelling, a senior member of the Bundesbank Council. Over the months, the Member States have, by different means and with varying degrees of success, been contorting themselves to reach convergence. Italy has levied swingeing taxes which they say they will repay later; France have shamelessly appropriated public sector pension fund monies worth billions: Germany froze Social Security benefits and cut public expenditure; Denmark reduced unemployment benefits; Belgium made welfare cuts; the Netherlands restricted housing benefits; Spain made the private sector responsible for unemployment insurance; Austria introduced austerity measures; and Sweden over a period of years imposed tax increases and public sector cuts; and other Member States have performed variations on the same theme.

These machinations are proving counter-productive, because they are causing widespread anger, increased unemployment, strikes, industrial unrest and general tension and disaffection. The manoeuvres are also self-defeating, because by the very nature of these "fudges", the convergence will not be **sustainable** (as required by Article 109j.1.) without increasing distortion and fudging.

Nevertheless, the Articles mentioned above contain such loose and undefined words as to make it easy for the Commission, with a nod and a wink, to decide that the criteria have been met. Article 104c 2 (a) and (b) are classic examples of Euro-drafting loaded with ambiguities, let-outs and escape routes.

Recognizing that the single currency is a needless and dangerous folly, it is worth thinking about the **cost** of it, including new machinery, electronic equipment, banknotes, coins, systems, and so on. Every company in the UK, (and in every other Member State) would have enormous expense in time and money. Marks & Spencer alone have estimated that their own introduction costs would amount to £100 million or more; and there are many thousands of companies, great and small, up and down the country, so the total would be countless billions. In addition to those costs, there would be, already are, the hidden costs of the distraction from running UK businesses and Government Departments caused by attending to the setting up and operation of the single currency. As an indicator, it is calculated that, for instance, the Ministry of Agriculture already has to spend some 70% of its time administering Commission Directives and Regulations. Also of course, the UK would be required to hand over most of its official foreign reserves, (Article 105.2), about £26 billion, to be held and managed by the European Central Bank (ECB) in Frankfurt on a non-returnable basis. This would be on top of the relatively less significant sum of £70 million already paid by the UK for the establishment of the ECB.

Chapter Four

IS THERE A BASIS FOR STAYING IN THE COMMUNITY?

Despite all the oppressive and fundamental drawbacks of the Community, the Government still express the hankering for the UK to be "at the heart of Europe", but on the other hand not to be in a Federal Union. They claim not to understand that this is a complete contradiction in terms and an objective which is impossible of achievement. Malcolm Rifkind said that the single currency was a "disaster waiting to happen", and that "jumping blindly towards ever greater integration" would lead to catastrophe. Lord Renton in 1995 attended a high-level conference on Legislation in the EC and made a confidential report on it to the Prime Minister and Douglas Hurd, the former Foreign Secretary. He reported a most unsatisfactory state of affairs; an "astonishing complexity and obscurity of the detailed contents of Directives and Regulations"; frequent failure to comply with EC laws on the part of France, Belgium, Italy, Spain, Portugal and Greece; the appalling difficulty of getting 15 countries with different languages and legal systems to agree on legislation. Lord Renton recommended that the Treaty should be scrapped and replaced; vast quantities of legislation should be repealed and not re-enacted; drastic cuts in the areas of EC law-making should be made; and if such steps are not taken, "the Community will become increasingly unworkable and chaotic". These are sensible findings, but available to anyone prepared to scratch the surface, so what have our Foreign Office and senior Government Ministers been doing all these years?

But there are other crucial matters which should be dealt with. The most vital is the need to remould the Commission into an ordinary administrative civil service **serving** the Council of Ministers and only producing draft legislation at the Council's request, with no power of **initiating** legislation. The concept of federal union should be abandoned and replaced by the Common Market between independent sovereign states. EMU and the single currency should be repudiated. The Common Fisheries Policy, non-existent in the Treaty of Rome, should be abolished. The Common Agricultural Policy should be drastically cut back or abolished. The Court of Auditors should be given much greater powers to enforce their findings and to police the massive fraud and corruption in connection with the payment of subsidies, Structural Funds and Cohesion Funds and to impose fines and other penalties. The European Court of Justice (ECJ) should be reconstituted as a proper Court of Law, staffed by fully qualified judges, instructed to have regard to the broad sweep of the law and not to act as an administrative agency merely enforcing the Treaty. The ECJ should not predominate over the highest courts of the Member States; and there should be a system of appeal from it to a superior court, perhaps the International Court at the Hague. Apart from purely Common Market matters, all other issues should revert to being dealt with by cooperation between independent sovereign Member States.

All these changes would require a new Treaty abrogating the Maastricht Treaty and the Single European Act and implementing these various points. The position outlined is what is needed by the UK, but we all know that there is not the slightest chance of achieving it. Jacques Santer said so in late April 1999, and made us aware yet again of the fateful ratchet of "acquis communautaire" clicking on, on, never back. So there are **no half measures**: it is **all or nothing**. The UK dislikes what there is, and hates what is to come, and it really must come to terms with the inescapable fact that it has no hope of negotiating an acceptable position. The federal juggernaut powered by the French-German axis thunders on. Struggle manfully as John Major might, his efforts really only won a stay of execution. Opt-outs tend to be temporary, and the Commission may well find dubious ways round them. In any event, opt-outs and other exceptions normally exact their toll by making us give concessions in other areas, and of course by worsening intra-Community relations.

Chapter Five

WHAT IF WE STAY IN, WITHOUT
THE CHANGES WE WANT?

The UK uses or threatens the use of the veto, or seeks opt-outs and exceptions, or delays, objects to and haggles over legislation, because it instinctively and fundamentally dislikes not only individual issues but also the whole framework and thrust of the Community. And the sad reality is that every time it does these things, it increasingly unites the other 14 Member States against us and engenders ever greater obduracy and bad feeling towards us. It may be that more recently there is a growing understanding, resentment and anger concerning the system amongst the **peoples** of the Community — there are strikes, rallies, civil and industrial unrest to bear witness to it — but the Community is scarcely democratic and the **Governments** are in the driving seat manoeuvring towards their federal ambition.

How will things develop? Gradually the veto will be eroded. In certain areas it may be conceded by us by way of compromise to achieve some perceived advantage. Gradually its reduction to extinction will occur as the Community enlarges to 20, 25 or even 30 Member States. Its existence will be harder and harder to defend or justify, the bigger and more unwieldy the Community grows.

The European Central Bank (ECB) (Articles 105-109, and Protocol), unaccountable and independent, will hold and manage our gold and other reserves of £26 billion, and dictate monetary policy, and impose fines and penalties on transgressors. Frankfurt was chosen as its base, despite London being by far the biggest and best exchange and investment centre in the whole of Europe, and with New York and Tokyo is one of the three biggest world financial centres. London carries out £190 billion foreign exchange dealings **per day**, some twenty times more than Frankfurt. The choice of Frankfurt is more strong evidence of the anti-Anglo-Saxon bias pervading the Community.

The Community as a trading bloc represents only some 15% of world markets and is falling behind the USA, the Pacific Basin and Latin America, and because of its "Fortress Europe" mentality this trend is likely to continue. The Institute of Directors has warned that many small UK companies risk being forced out of business by the high cost of meeting EC requirements for product standardization and certification.

The CAP will continue to featherbed the farmers of France and Germany, and it will become ever more costly, to accommodate Poland and other Eastern European countries as they join the Community.

Always a thorny problem, making Community food prices some 70% above the world level, it may increase to the point of collapse amid confusion, destabilization of markets, infighting and ill-will.

The CFP is causing fury and bankruptcy in the UK fishing fleet and industry. Our centuries-old traditional fishing waters will be ever more diminished among the other Member States, and further again when enlargement of the Community takes place. Quota-hopping is a vast irritant, and various forms of cheating are rife, for instance, with the Spanish and French using illegally small-holed nets. This will continue, with fish stocks being ravaged and gradually extinguished.

There are already numerous Commission Directives concerning VAT, and there will be more, as part of the move towards general tax harmonization. This harmonization implies that eventually common tax regimes will be introduced including income, capital, consumption and social insurance tax rates. It will not be long before two VAT bands are installed, and books, newspapers, food, childrens clothes, public transport, and house purchase are brought into the net. VAT on food alone would cost the UK an estimated extra £7 billion a year.

Other new areas of regulation provided for by Maastricht are:

Education (Article 126-7); Culture (Article 128); Public Health (Article 129); Consumer Protection (Article 129a); Trans-European networks in the areas of transport, telecommunications and energy infrastructures (Article 129 b-d); Industry (Article 130); and Development Co-operation (Article 130 u-y). Relentless pursuit of interference by the Commission in those areas will of course impose huge cost burdens on Member States and add greatly to the already heavy demands on the Community Budget.

This Budget has already taken an estimated £30 billion from the UK in **net** contributions at current prices, and we are the second largest net contributors (after Germany). Unless the Court of Auditors is given much wider powers, the annual loss of at least £5-6 billion wasted through fraud will continue, and maybe increase, unchecked.

The Western European Union (WEU), founded in 1948 as a defence group and comprising the majority of Community Members, will be in line for development, probably to the detriment of NATO. Such a manoeuvre would reflect the antipathy of several Member States, particularly France and Germany, towards the "Anglo-Saxon" USA which is the main force in NATO.

Efforts will be made to create a common foreign policy (Article J), though only a complete fantasist could expect 15, and later more, countries totally different from each other in every respect to have a unanimous stance in this field. Examples are there for all to see: "Germany's Balkan Folly" in the recognition of Croatia and Slovenia; Zaïre; Albania; Germany breaking ranks regarding Iran, so as to preserve its trade with that country: France not joining in a Human Rights tentative to China, so as to protect its trade with that country. Many more cases will arise.

What other horrors are round the corner? In the ruthless distortion of nationhood in the onrush to federalism, many undesirable and hugely expensive steps will be taken. For instance, in the transport network field, the UK may be required to conform by **driving on the righthand side of the road**. A moment's thought shows that this upheaval would cost many billions in road signs over every yard of the entire UK. Continental heavier lorries will necessitate repaired or new roads, reinforced bridges, and so on — more billions. Commissioner Ripa di Meana once proposed a major road right through Snowdonia National Park, so as to facilitate traffic between Ireland and the continent.

Fisheries were from Heath's notorious concession in 1972 onwards a "common European resource", so, worryingly, it may be difficult to resist the approach to designate our rich North Sea **oil and gas** assets as a "common resource". This would cost us untold billions. Oil and gas and fisheries must have been leading reasons why Norway had the enormous good sense to stay out of the Community.

Another huge danger mark at some point in time is the vast sums which will be needed to fund the **continental unfunded pensions**. The UK will be dragged into this and be required to pay large sums into this bottomless pit.

As reported (*The Daily Telegraph* 30th April 1997) the French Commissioner in charge of monetary union Yves Thibault de Silguy in Washington addressing the Group of Seven industrial nations — of which the UK is a founder member — proposed that G7 should be superseded by G3, representing the interests of the dollar, the yen and the euro, with the euro being represented by the President of the European Central Bank. This would deprive the UK of its seat on G7, and further enhance the power of the ECB. This is yet another clear sign of the unstoppable advance of federalism in the Community, of which there is more and more evidence on a daily basis.

The Community's **Committee of the Regions** is stealthily forwarding its programme. This Committee is recognized by Article 198 and its Protocol, and has a special Directorate-General, XVI, in the Commission to work for it. The Committee has 222 members drawn from local and regional authorities and is ostensibly "the natural guarantor of 'subsidiarity', the principle that decisions should be taken by public authorities at a level as close as possible to the citizen"; (Inter-institutional Directory European Union, page 341).

In fact, the hidden objective is to break up the nations of the Community, nation by nation, and link each region directly to Brussels and so bypass and marginalize the national governments. Labour's plan to give Wales and Scotland their own Assemblies is playing straight into Brussel's hands. The Commission's map shows England divided into eight Euro-regions. In September 1995 at a closed meeting in Chichester between representatives from the Commission and councils in Sussex and Kent, the promotion of regional identity was discussed. The Commission's blueprint is to establish **regions bestriding existing national boundaries**, so as to diminish national control and identity. Thus West Sussex, East Sussex and Kent are seen forming **one** Euro-region with Nord-Pas-de-Calais, Haute Normandie and Picardie. The map also hints at the Channel Islands being joined with Basse Normandie as a possible Euro-region. An early example of the cross-border region is the Schleswig-Slesvig Euro-region on the Danish-German border.

How far the Commission will go in seeking to re-align national territories is not known. The map of the Committee of the Regions also shows Northern Ireland's Ulster and the Republic of Ireland's Donegal as one new cross-border Euro-region. In another sphere, one may expect Spain to step up its pressure to recover Gibraltar, pressure directly on the UK but also indirectly through Brussels.

Enlargement of the Community by the Eastern European countries will surely come about in a few years' time and the Community will likewise become a Federal Union. On the fall of the Berlin Wall in 1989 Chancellor Kohl declared: "We want European Union, the United States of Europe". Enlargement will naturally bring enormous problems and maybe dangers. Eastern Europe is by recent history communist or communist-dominated, and for the most part industrially poor and mainly agricultural. This will provide huge and serious difficulties for the CAP. Independent Reports commissioned by the Community estimated the increased cost would be between £10 billion and £25 billion, doubling its cost to the existing Member States. New "enlarging" States will presumably be entitled to a share of the UK's fishing waters, thus further reducing our share and draining the declining stocks, and also a share of any other "common European resources" identified and annexed by the Commission. Whether these new Member States will be able to squeeze into the straitjacket of the convergence criteria, and sustain that position, is impossible to say. Nor can one predict the difficulties and dangers surrounding security, immigration, defence and foreign policy problems. The differences between the 15 current Member States are countless and well nigh unbridgeable, so the "enlarging" countries will add an immeasurable dimension.

Our aim is the end of the nation State
Former President Herzog of Germany

There can be no doubt that a **Federal Union** will come about, under a Constitution replacing the Treaties. The European Parliament's Report in 1993 on the Draft Constitution said that the latter "would foster clarity and truth by putting an end to the fiction of the abiding intact sovereignty of the Member States...". In a lecture at the House of Commons in April 1996 Bernard Connolly highlighted the implacable and irresistible momentum of the federalists towards Union which he described as madness. Connolly was a senior British official in the Commission from 1978 to 1996, and since 1989 he was head of the division dealing with the ERM and monetary policy affairs. Gradually over these years he came to realize that the ERM and EMU were "a massive lie" and "part of a programme to subvert the independence — political as well as economic — of Europe's countries". He wrote a book entitled *The Rotten Heart of Europe* sounding the alert against the system and was promptly dismissed from the Commission, and treated by it, in Orwellian terms, as a "thought criminal" and an "unperson".

European federation has been the long-term underlying aim of the French-German axis and the Benelux countries since 1950. Roy Denman, a former senior British Commission official who "went native" in Brussels and supported federation, speciously drew a parallel with Switzerland and the USA, but these are obviously false analogies. Switzerland has been a Confederation of small, closely clustered cantons for the last 700 years. The history of the USA as a separate nation goes back only some 200 years, but it has always been one country formed of an increasing number of States which had no former independent international existence. Incidentally, the countries forming the North American Free Trade Area (NAFTA) led by the USA do not have a single currency and manage very well without one. Walter Hallstein, President of the Commission from 1958 to 1967 said: "Any nation which comes into the Common Market is accepting a far-reaching **political** commitment". In 1965 he said: "Unification ... aims at a new ordering of **all political power** in Europe". At the time of the Rome Summit meeting in October 1990 Jacques Delors unveiled proposals for a politically united Europe, wherein the European Parliament would be the Community's "House of Representatives", the Council of Ministers would be "the Senate", and Delors' Commission under his Presidency would form the new government of a "United States of Europe". On 23rd January 1991 in his address to the European Parliament Delors outlined this programme of progress towards political and economic union.

Many leading figures in the Community, too numerous to refer to here, have over the last 40 years been speaking of the federal ambition, but almost as if by conspiracy, little or no mention of this has been made available in the UK until the last very few years. A report revealed (*Sunday Telegraph*, 17th April 1997) a secretly funded unit of the Foreign Office with close links to MI6 conducting a covert propaganda operation aimed at ensuring the UK joined the Community. The operation by the Foreign Office Information Research Department (IRD) was set up in 1948 to counter communist propaganda at the start of the Cold War and had a long-term programme of private meetings between pro-European politicians, diplomats, businessmen and senior figures in broadcasting and the press. This campaign helped swing public opinion in favour of our entry into the Common Market. Norman Reddaway, a senior Foreign Office official, ran this IRD covert operation and the report named a number of politicians and media men who were fed pro-Europe propaganda for transmission in broadcast programmes. This was found useful by some, as "there was a paucity of facts about the EEC". This unattractive secrecy on the part of the Foreign Office and successive Governments over decades is an arrogant denial of democracy and an abuse of authority.

When the Federal Union comes, as it certainly will, the once great UK will be reduced to the status of an outlying province, or a "rate-capped county council", in Norman Ridley's stark but discerning words. The sheet-anchor of the veto will be eroded to extinction in the course of the Amsterdam and later Summits, and as enlargement proceeds, all the current difficulties will be multiplied and exacerbated. The inflated CAP will create insupportable burdens for all involved and then probably collapse. The CFP will disastrously lead to the virtual extinction of fish stocks in the present Community fishing waters, with accompanying fury and risk of violence. The single currency and monetary policy dictated by the ECB at Frankfurt will build up impossible strains on the disparate economies of all the very different Member States, creating more and more unemployment, civil and industrial unrest and bitter hostility and ill-feeling on all sides. The Community budget will continue not to be approved by the Court of Auditors, but without any repercussions. Widespread, massive fraud and corruption will go on draining the budget; again the Court of Auditors will record the fact, and nothing will be done about it. NATO will be diminished in favour of the WEU, in accordance with the Community's anti-Anglo-Saxon prejudice, but at increased risk to the security and defence of Greater Europe. Without national controls, immigration will become an even greater source of civil instability, difficulty and aggravation. The Structural and Cohesion Funds (Article 130b and d, and Protocol) used for supporting the poorer countries will be strained, to the point of placing impossible financial burdens on the main contributors to the budget. Attempts at unified foreign policy (Article J) will continue to cut across the varying national interests of trade and influence of all but the smallest Member States, and those attempts will founder amid fury and recrimination. And this is just a glimpse of what is to come. For the truth is that even to attempt to put 15, 20 or 30 totally different countries into the melting pot and render them down into one homogenized entity is dangerously lunatic. Charlemagne, Napoleon, Hitler — their empires all failed to outlive them. The French-German axis, with their satellites in tow, and the poor ancillary countries anxious for their Community welfare payments, will strangle each other in their embrace.

Turning from the total subordination and dependence of a Member of a European Federal Union, to the position of **a State of the USA** highlights an interesting contrast. Under the American Constitution there are specific distinctions between the Federal and the State positions. Each State has its own defined areas of legislation and control, with which the Federal Government cannot interfere. Various aspects of taxation, education, policing, criminal law, transport, health, planning and other matters are all within the field of State governance, beyond the reach of the federal machine.

Also, in the USA at Federal level they have the three-sided control of checks and balances of the President and his office, the Congress and the Supreme Court. At State level a similar system applies, of State Governor, State legislature and State Supreme Court. By contrast, in the Community there will be the Commission as the Government, acting with very little check or hindrance, because the European Parliament has limited powers and influence and the Court of Justice is no more than an administrative agency enforcing the Treaty. European countries would have more independence and self-governance as a State of the USA than as a Member of the planned European Federal Union.

Chapter Six

WHAT IF WE COME OUT OF
THE COMMUNITY?

There are many obvious, immediate and enormous advantages, and there are also some areas of less certainty. What is astonishing is that over all these years no Government or independent research body has prepared a **cost/benefit analysis** of the whole position. There are suspicious or doubting countries — Norway and Switzerland decided against the Community, Greenland went in and left, Denmark said "no" once and then had its arm twisted. The people of France voted very narrowly to join. UK surveys now show substantial numbers who wish to come out.

Looking at some of the **obvious advantages to withdrawal**, cessation of CAP costs would release billions for reinvestment in the NHS or elsewhere, and would free each household from the cost of some £1,040 a year, which would be the saving if food were bought on world markets. The Common Fisheries Policy would end for the UK, we could regain our territorial waters, previously agreed internationally, we could rebuild our fishing fleets and give rebirth to that once thriving industry. We would not have to hand over our gold and foreign reserves to the ECB. We would preserve the pound sterling, and govern our own interest rates and all forms of direct and indirect taxation. Our Parliament would be our supreme lawmaker. Our Government would be free to govern. Our system of supreme Courts would be supreme again, and not be subordinate to that group of administrative bureaucratic enforcers of the Treaty on the ECJ. We could save the massive cost (or that part not already wasted) of preparing for the single currency — the estimated cost to UK retailing alone is £22 billion. Our Ministries and Government Departments would be able to give their full attention to UK business, instead of having to spend high proportions of their time giving effect to Brussels legislation. Our political parties could heal their wounds and get on with UK affairs. Many of our small businesses would be able to re-start or improve, free from the dead hand of product standardization and certification and all the other inhibitions of alien legislation. We would be safe from restrictive legislation in the new fields opened up in the Maastricht Treaty. Our oil and gas resources could not be pillaged from us by being treated as "common resources". We could not later be burdened with funding the bottomless pit of Community unfunded pensions.

I believe we could look forward to our trading future with confidence, and indeed with growing confidence. We will of course go on trading all over Europe, as we have done for centuries, and Community countries will undoubtedly wish to go on trading with us. We would also want to continue trading with former members of the European Free Trade Area (EFTA) such as Norway and Switzerland. And we would continue and foster our trade with our Commonwealth partners all over the world, with the USA, Latin America, the Pacific basin and China. We should remind ourselves that the Organization for Economic Co-operation and Development (OECD), the International Monetary Fund (IMF) and the World Bank all see the UK as a success story. We would work to maintain and improve the City's position as the top European foreign exchange and investment centre, and also to encourage and boost ever more inward investment, from countries who welcome our advantages of favourable labour market, our long experience, expertise and many contacts in world markets, and our English language, the language of the airways, the seaways and the prime language of commerce.

As mentioned, Community trade is in the slow track, accounting for only some 15% of world trade, and gradually losing world market share. It is suffering from **Euro-atrophy**, a wasting disease the federal strain of which may prove terminal, and the UK could quicken its pace if it discarded the EC shackles.

We are now just before the Amsterdam Summit and Maastricht

II, when a series of further developments down the path towards federal union will be decided. At such a time, and before summit negotiations of any future Treaties, it is useful to halt for a moment to **review in panorama the course of the last 40 years**: the structure and institutions of the Community are the natural offspring of the dirigiste bureaucratic socialist mind-set which pervades much of Europe; the conspiratorial secrecy of the Commission, which is unsavoury, in contempt of democracy, and redolent with deception; the unshakeable and irresistible momentum towards the goal of Federal integration, the secret agenda all along, ar.d always underestimated in the UK; the whole series of measures indivisibly and seamlessly linked together leading from one Summit Meeting to the next; the fact that the single currency and monetary union are not necessary economically, but are a **political** manoeuvre to bind Member States into a "single institutional framework", the Federal Union; the fact that the engine of the Community is the French-German axis; the paradox that whilst the French-German axis, apparently united, provides the motive power and in effect takes all the main decisions, France and Germany are the arch-rivals fighting powerfully throughout for supremacy and domination; the increasingly obvious fact that the longer the UK stays in the Community, vainly trying to "negotiate", the more we become securely and ruinously entrapped in the quagmire of federalism; from all this, it must be clearly understood that the objective of a Federal Union, with one Constitution, one Government (the Commission), one Parliament, and one Central Bank is quite simply **non-negotiable**.

Our Government must not sink our nationhood in the murky and turbulent waters of abandoned sovereignty. We must be **Anglocentric**, and not ECcentric. This is no time for ECcentricity.

POSTSCRIPT

I write in elegiac mood, after the landslide victory of Labour in the General Election. This mood is because, whatever the many mistakes and misunderstandings regarding the Community by all our Governments over the years since our entry in 1972-3 and before, right up to the present, the new Labour Government is set to embrace the Social Chapter, is sympathetic to the UK's joining the single currency and the Economic and Monetary Union, and may prove to be even more accommodating in other ways. This stance will accelerate our progress towards being **a mere dependency** in the Federal Union.

LIST OF READING AND REFERENCE

1. "The Maastricht consolidated Treaty on European Union" (June 1992) British Management Data Foundation.

2. "The Unseen Treaty" (April-September 1992).

3. "The Convoluted Treaties-II-Rome 1957" Nelson, Pollard & Wheeler.

4. "EC Treaties 1987".

5. "The Constitution of the European Union (September 1993), Working Document and Draft Report by a European Parliament Committee".

6. "There is an alternative" (1996) Burkitt, Baimbridge and Whyman.

7. "The Castle of Lies" (1996) Booker and North.

8. "The Mad Officials" (1994) Booker and North.

9. "The Rotten Heart of Europe" (1995) Bernard Connolly.

10. "The Times Guide to the Single European Market" (1992) Owen and Dynes.

11. "The Rape of Britannia" (1992) Jack Obdam.

12. "From Rome to Maastricht" (1992) Burkitt, Baimbridge & Reed.

13. "The European Community" (1991) Budd & Jones.

14. "The Trap" (1993) James Goldsmith.

15. "Europe as 1996 Approaches" (May 1994) Rodney Leach.

16. "The European Journal", monthly editions.

17. "Europeople" (1992) Tony Gray.

18. "Inter-institutional Directory", European Union (423 pages).

PART II

DEFEATISM OR RESURGENCE?

Maelstrom: A whirlpool; a confused disordered state of affairs; any resistless overpowering influence for destruction.

Vortex: A whirlpool, a pursuit, way of life, situation, etc. that engulfs one irresistibly or remorselessly, taking up all one's attention or energies.

PART II

DEFEATISM OR RESURGENCE?

CONTENTS

Chapter One

A BRIEF TOUR D'HORIZON

Since the Labour Government came to power it has relinquished the UK's hard-won opt-out from the Social Chapter and accepted the regulations concerning minimum wages and working hours. It has not at present adopted the single currency, but is mounting an extensive campaign preparing the country for a referendum on the subject and for joining when it thinks the economic conditions are right. The single currency has been adopted by eleven Member States, although several of them only met the convergence criteria by various forms of financial and fiscal distortion and fudging. Wim Duisenberg was eventually appointed as the President of the unaccountable European Central Bank, after a furious and intense wrangle centred round the French who were extremely keen for their man Jean-Claude Trichet to get the job. The Euro was launched on 1st January 1999 and has steadily weakened against sterling and the dollar. The Treaty of Amsterdam was signed in October 1997 and came into effect in May 1999, extending the Maastricht Treaty in various ways, and strengthening the Commission and the EP in the inexorable progress towards federal union. A report following an investigation into widespread corruption, nepotism and fraud in the handling of EU budgetary funds produced damning evidence involving a number of Commissioners. In January 1999 the EP notably failed to use its powers to call the Commission to account, but it rallied in March to exert sufficient pressure to cause all twenty Commissioners to resign en bloc. The EU Members of NATO went along, with varying degrees of reluctance and material support, with the large-scale NATO bombing war in the Kosovo conflict, although the expedition as a whole seemed to be of dubious legitimacy. Trade skirmishes have taken place between the EU and the USA concerning bananas and beef, although it is hoped that the threat of escalation has subsided. For the rest, matters have continued much as before, for instance: Member States have failed to agree changes to the EU Budget; no progress was made in amending the Common Agricultural Policy; the Commission continues to pour out a stream of intrusive legislation; the European Court of Justice is as determined as ever to reinforce and extend the ambit and powers of Community institutions under the Treaties; EU waste and fraud, regularly identified by the Court of Auditors but hitherto uncorrected, seems to continue unchecked; and as ever, all the diverse national interests are relentlessly fought for, often entailing much bad feeling. Plus ça change....

Chapter Two

THE CONSTANT MANOEUVRE
TOWARDS FEDERAL UNION

The people must be led slowly and unconsciously...
Pamphlet *Design for Europe*, Peter Thorneycroft, 1947

Europe will be your revenge
Said by Chancellor Adenauer to President
de Gaulle after the Suez debacle in 1956

I want first to highlight the stark contrast between on the one hand
the intention repeatedly expressed over the last fifty years in
Government circles in continental Europe to work towards
integration and federal union, of which intention UK Government
circles have been aware, and on the other hand the almost universal
ignorance of that intention on the part of the **public at large**.

How this degree of ignorance has come about or been achieved
is very difficult to understand. A central factor is, I believe, that by
character our island people, independent for a thousand years, have
little or no interest in politics and no desire to follow or try to
understand the Byzantine processes and manoeuvres of continental
and Community politics but nevertheless have a strong innate
aversion to their sovereign country being emasculated and
demeaned to the level of a mere province, or "rate-capped county
council". This innate aversion will remain, though the people have
so far not been alerted to the creeping danger of federalization, but
they must be roused as soon as possible, before it is too late.

Even so, it is a baffling enigma. Ever since television became
widespread, that medium has been the most dominant one,
although radio still plays its part. I know of no person or group

fully aware of the federal goal and wanting to spell out the dangers for the UK who is allowed air-time. It seems as if in some ways and at times the BBC is scarcely more than an arm of Government, and that it has been influenced by the Foreign Office and the European Movement. The latter strongly pro-integration propaganda body has since 1948 been moling away, funded by Brussels and reportedly by the Government, the USA and perhaps others. Its main targets are politicians, officials, producers, editors and journalists in the media, the CBI and the City and business world, and academics, and it seems that its quietly unremitting activities have borne fruit.

Unfortunately there has not been, at any rate so far, any countervailing group with comparable funding and support to spread public awareness at a broad national level of the dangers and drawbacks of the federal integrationist course.

Part of this enigma can perhaps be attributable to the fact that the EU is in essence undemocratic, with the great engines of its government — the Commission, the European Central Bank, and the European Court of Justice — unelected and unaccountable. Therefore in the case of the UK with its long history of freedom, independence and parliamentary government, it is easy, though distasteful, to see why a series of our Governments have thought it expedient to be **secretive, deceitful and untruthful** on the subject of the federal goal, in their sly progress towards downgrading their sovereign country to a mere **province** in a factious group run by a dirigiste bureaucracy. I have commented on the deceitfulness of this secrecy, which is a most flagrant and overbearing abuse of democracy. I have to say that I find this long-running betrayal of the British people by its various Governments utterly disgraceful, and one may envisage that in earlier times the piecemeal surrender of national sovereignty to another power would for the perpetrators have ended on the block.

Dirigiste bureaucracy is the antithesis of democracy and is a common factor between Communist, Socialist, as well as Nazi, Vichyite and Fascist regimes. A well documented book *The Tainted*

Source by John Laughland (1998) discusses some links between
Nazi, Vichyite and Fascist thought in the 1930s and early 1940s,
and the ideology of European integration of present times. The
main founding fathers of the Community, Jean Monnet, Robert
Schuman, Paul-Henri Spaak and Alcide de Gasperi, at some time
Ministers or Prime Ministers of their own countries which had
centralized bureaucratic Government in the socialist/communist
style, were naturally going to create a monolithic structure in the
same mould.

Thus federal union has been the central objective ever since the
late 1940s (and maybe before) of the original Six, and subsequently
of the further continental Members. For fifty years federalism was
the secret agenda, initially camouflaged by the drive for a Common
Market which was held out as the ostensible objective. The degree
of secrecy vis à vis **the public at large** about the true goal on the
part of the Commission and continental leaders was very marked
right up to the 1990s, and on the part of the UK Government it
continues up to the present.

It must be remembered that on the continent, at Community and
Government level, the position has been **constant and unswerving**
to make all efforts towards federal union. In the UK, at
Government level, the attitude has been one of **frequent shifts and
vacillation**, without apparently ever a proper grasp of the full
significance and implications. In the Community, the Treaties have
of course been the main milestones (to be referred to in the next
chapter), but in between them were other tentatives to accelerate the
process. For instance, there was the Fouchet Plan of 1961, for
economic and political union and joint foreign policy; the Werner
Plan of 1970, for economic and monetary union by 1980; and the
Leo Tindemans Plan of 1976 for the Fouchet and Werner aims and
also common regional, social and industrial progress. These and
other initiatives, though they failed, had a knock-on effect. As to
individuals on the continent, the list of names at Community and
government level proclaiming their common goal is endless, and I

mention only a few. It goes without saying that Jean Monnet and Robert Schuman, two of the founding fathers, were steadfast federalists. However, Jean Monnet was not really interested in the Common Market concept, although that was the initial chosen vehicle. In 1950 Robert Schuman, French Foreign Minister and former Vichy Minister, announced the launch of the European Coal and Steel Community (the precursor of the EEC) and in his speech stated the French-German objective as being to "provide for the setting up of a common base for economic development as a first step in the **federation of Europe**". Walter Hallstein, President of the Commission (1958-67) said that: "Any nation which comes into the Common Market is accepting a far-reaching **political** commitment". Also, in a speech in 1965 he said, "Unification is not confined to individual sectors of the public life of Europe, but aims at a **new ordering of all political power in Europe**".

During the next twenty years the leaders in the Community were taking the same line. In the 1980s the arch-bureaucratic federalist Jacques Delors, President of the Commission, was focusing and strengthening the drive for integration. In July 1988 Delors told the European Parliament: "In ten years, 80% of the laws on the economy and social policy will be passed at a European and not at national level. We are not going to manage to take all the decisions needed between now and 1995 unless we see the beginnings of a **European Government**". In January 1990 Delors said: "My objective is that before the end of the millennium Europe should have a **true federation**". On the completion of the Maastricht Treaty Chancellor Kohl said: "The European Union Treaty introduces a new and decisive stage in the process of European Union which within a few years will lead to the creation of what the founding fathers of modern Europe dreamed of after the last war, **the United States of Europe**". Again, in 1993 Delors said: "we're not here just to make a single market, but **a political union**".

Increasingly during the 1990s Community leaders have ever more clearly been spelling out the federal goal.

Here are a few instances:

*The process of monetary union goes hand in hand, must go
hand in hand, with political integration and ultimately
political union. EMU is, and always was meant to be,
a stepping stone on the way to a united Europe*
Wim Duisenberg, the Dutch President of the European Central Bank

Monetary union is the motor of European integration
Belgian Prime Minister, Jean-Luc Dehaene

*The single currency is the greatest abandonment of sovereignty since
the foundation of the European Community... It is a decision of an
essentially political nature. We need this **United Europe** ... we
must never forget that the Euro is an instrument for this project*
May 1998, Felipe Gonzales, former Prime Minister of Spain

*A signal must be sent ... that a single market and a
single currency is not the end of the EU journey*
October 1998, Viktor Klima, Chancellor of Austria

*We ought to work on a common **Constitution** to turn the
European Union into an entity under international law ... that
is my goal. It is the decisive task of our time*
November 1998, Joschka Fischer, Foreign Minister of Germany

*The single currency was the theme of the Nineties. We
must now face the difficult task of moving towards
a single economy, a **single political unity***
April 1999, Romano Prodi, President of the European Commission
and former Italian Prime Minister

Integration and federal union have been the common theme and
goal of Presidents of the Commission over time. The two recent

Presidents, Jacques Delors and then Jacques Santer were prominent exponents of the theme since at least the mid-1980s. Now Romano Prodi, whose appointment was backed by Blair, is already declaring his fervent determination to pursue the federal goal. As further steps on this path, he said: "We must try to achieve real harmonization of our economic systems", with harmonization of tax early on the agenda. As part of the same process, he says, "Amsterdam and Maastricht need to be followed by a Treaty that will give us our own defence capabilities". Germany who held the EU Presidency for the first half of 1999 are pressing for a "Bill of Rights" which it sees in the longer term as forming the cornerstone of a **Constitution for Europe**. Joschka Fischer the German Foreign Minister is stressing the essential need for Member States to surrender more sovereignty, reduce national vetoes and reform Community finances and institutions, in preparation for enlargement to the East. **"Political union** must be our lodestar from now on", he says. German leaders and top officials are widely proclaiming the need to harmonize VAT and Corporation Tax and querying the need for Member States to continue to have national foreign ministers, diplomatic services and armies.

The intention to achieve federal union expressed by leaders all over Europe over decades has broken cover and reached a crescendo in recent years.

I will now take a look at the perceptions and attitudes of some of our leaders and officials on this side of the channel over the last fifty years. In 1946-8 Churchill in his speeches showed interest in a United States of Europe, but not for the UK to be part of it. In 1950 the UK refused to join the European Coal and Steel Community (ECSC) promoted by Monnet and Schuman, and in December 1951 a Foreign Office policy document stated that the UK "cannot consider submitting our political and economic system to supranational institutions".

Throughout the whole post-war period the France-Germany axis has always been, and continues to be, the engine of the developing federal union, and so it is unlikely that in the run-up to the Treaty of Rome in 1956-57 the UK could have altered the federal course or the socialist bureaucratic institutions being developed on the Continent, even if it had wanted to do so. The merger (or cession) of sovereignty was an underlying theme even then.

Indeed, the Eden Government did not attend the Messina Conference in 1955 but sent an observer, Russell Bretherton, a Board of Trade official. Bretherton is quoted (*The Daily Telegraph*, 3rd December 1998) as addressing the Conference thus: "The future Treaty which you are discussing has no chance of being agreed; if it is agreed, it would have no chance of being ratified; if it was ratified, it would have no chance of being applied. And if it was applied, it would be totally unacceptable to Britain. You speak of agriculture, which we don't like, of power over customs, which we take exception to, and of institutions, which frighten us. Monsieur le Président, messieurs, au revoir et bonne chance".

In July 1960 the Cabinet Secretary, Sir Norman Brook, produced a Report referring to sovereignty questions and federalism and to the fact of "some progressive loss of sovereignty over a number of matters". In 1962 Hugh Gaitskill the Labour Leader expressed the view that for the UK to enter into the federation which the Community was seeking would make us a mere **"province"** in the **United States of Europe**. At Gaitskill's instigation, Harold Wilson set up a committee including Dennis Healey, James Callaghan, Douglas Jay and Peter Shore who considered a memorandum by John Murray. This paper indicated a "very serious erosion of sovereignty" and asked whether we were giving away our political birthright under the guise of a trading relationship.

According to the eminent historian, the late Lord Beloff, by 1964 when the Wilson Government took office, Whitehall had largely become pro-Community, as it was to remain. In 1966 Con O'Neill returned to the Foreign Office after serving as ambassador to the EEC, and produced a pro-EEC briefing which led to the setting up of the **European Integration Unit** in the Foreign Office. This formed the F.O. stance from then on. In 1967, a Cabinet meeting had a paper from Sir Burke Trend and other top officials to the effect that the UK had no future except within the Community. Douglas Jay in his book *Change and Fortune* asked the question why most of the British Establishment during the 1960s did a "**somersault**" to embrace a policy which placed a heavy financial burden on us, lowered our standard of living, weakened our influence, and damaged Parliament's control over our affairs.

In 1966 Edward Heath said in the House of Commons that the Community would involve surrender of sovereignty. And Heath's own biographer admitted that Parliament in 1971 and the country in 1975 were **hoodwinked** into signing up for more than they were ever told. Even the pro-European former civil servant Sir Roger Tomkys wrote that the Labour Government's referendum of 1975 was a **fraud** by civil servants and Government to keep the UK in the Community and to conceal as far as possible the **disadvantages of membership**. Heath gave a helping hand to the 1975 Labour referendum campaign by saying: "There is no question of any erosion of essential national sovereignty", although he knew that this was not true.

Over the last fifty years in the UK, various Governments, political leaders, Ministers and civil servants have **changed views** about the desirability of the UK being a member of the Community, and in both the main political parties there have been those for, and against, membership or at least, federation.

Churchill (Tory) and Eden (Tory) were against, Macmillan (Tory) was for, Gaitskill (Labour) was against, Wilson (Labour) was for, Heath (Tory) was for, Callaghan (Labour) was against, Douglas Jay (Labour) and Peter Shore (Labour) were against, Roy Jenkins (Labour) and George Brown (Labour) were for, Tony Benn (Labour) was for until 1964 and against by and after 1971, Barbara Castle (Labour) was against, but changed to being for on becoming an MEP, Kinnock (Labour) was against until he became a EU Commissioner, John Smith (Labour) was for, Kenneth Clarke

(Tory), Michael Heseltine (Tory) and Geoffrey Howe (Tory) were all for and so on, up to the present. A bald "for" or "against" is of course a gross oversimplification; there are many shades between black and white, and many more shifts of belief (or at least of support) than I have indicated.

Over the years there have been deep divisions over Europe in both the Labour and Conservative **parties**. In the 1950s and early 1960s the Labour Party were anti-Community, but by the mid-1960s they changed their policy, and it was the Wilson Government whose application to join the Community was rejected by President de Gaulle in 1967. At the time of the 1975 referendum, the Labour Government was still pro-Community, but by 1980 the Labour Party's annual conference **voted for unconditional withdrawal from the Community**, and in the 1983 election they campaigned for the withdrawal course to be followed. However, under John Smith's leadership they soon changed again to being pro-Community.

On the Conservative side, Churchill's and Eden's Governments between 1951-57 were against joining the Community, but with the "wind of change" Macmillan's Government wanted to join, although it was kept out in 1961-63 by de Gaulle with the backing of the Commission. Heath took us into the Treaty of Rome in 1972 with all its drawbacks, costs and handicaps. Thatcher was hoodwinked by the Foreign Office into signing the Single European Act in 1986, but she obviously had no wish for federalism, as evidenced by her Bruges speech in 1988. John Major had hallucinations of the UK being "at the very heart of Europe" whilst remaining an independent sovereign nation state.

This brief outline shows that the concept of the political goal of federalism has been the **constant** motif in the Community for at least fifty years, and that this has been **known** in UK Government and official circles for most if not all of that time. The disturbing peculiarity is that, as if by some masonic conspiracy of silence, this position has not been made known to the British **public** by successive Governments who have followed the shaming and deceitful "slowly and unconsciously" principle. It seems probable that the same has been the case on the continent as well, at least up to the 1990s, by which time the Treaty of Maastricht and more recently the Treaty of Amsterdam have made the federal objective more and more apparent. However, the public at large do not read Treaties.

In the UK, Government ministers and officials have remained mute or dismissive about the federal goal, though exceptionally Heath in July 1990 referred in Parliament, though not openly to the public, to the UK being a mere "unit" in a federal system. In September 1989 the Chancellor Nigel Lawson discounted plans for a single currency, saying it would lead to a "United States of Europe". However, "That is not on the agenda", he said. In September 1993 John Major said that "the mantra of full economic and monetary union" has "all the quaintness of a rain dance", and Kenneth Clarke said the project had a "snowball's chance in Hades". These postures of ignorance, disbelief or concealment in the face of all the evidence are surely curious and perplexing, as well as profoundly irritating.

For the rest, any criticism, discussion or even mention of federalism was and still is treated as an eccentricity, a neurosis or a mental fixation. Up until two years ago, and maybe still, Kenneth Clarke described the concern about federalism as "paranoid nonsense". However, in the face of the mountain of evidence of the federal intention, it is those who deny or ignore it who appear to be the victims of paranoia. Interestingly, in spite of his dismissive remark about fears of federalism, Kenneth Clarke said in the House of Commons in July 1971: "Economic and monetary union, political development, a common foreign policy, a defence policy, international contacts all this lies in the future of the Community".

The quarantined minds of most UK leaders have not caught the contagion of federalism, but even those infected do not understand the virus. Since coming to power in May 1997, Blair has confirmed his allegiance and embraced a new era of deeper European integration, although he said he is seeking to keep certain policies the preserve of national governments. It is of interest to recall that in 1975 Blair voted for the UK to remain in the EEC, but that in April 1982 he expressed the view that: "Above all, the EEC takes away Britain's freedom to follow the economic policies we need", and that: "**I support withdrawal from the EEC** (certainly unless the most fundamental changes are effected)". Politicians' volte-faces are hardly rare, the proper kind are made for good reasons in the national interest, and the kind to be condemned are made to suit the party line and the individual's own career objectives.

Chapter Three

THE TREATIES, MORE AND MORE

Words, words, words
Hamlet

*With inky blots and rotten parchment bonds, that England that
was wont to conquer others, hath made a shameful conquest of itself*
Richard II

The federal concept has been the continental goal throughout, but
this was largely concealed from the **public in the Treaty of Rome,
1957**, and ever since. Indeed, much of UK Government and
Establishment seemed to be sceptical or uncomprehending. It is
worth pointing out right away a significant difference between the
legal drafting of Treaties on the continent and similar Parliamentary
drafting in the UK (to be more precise, under the law of England),
as regards **Preambles**. Neither in the UK nor on the continent are
Preambles legally binding, but they carry less weight in UK Acts. In
the Community, the Preamble is written **after** the Treaty has been
formulated and outlines the decisions and the aspirations and
political intentions of the participating countries, both as
represented in that Treaty and also **as a guide for future action**.
The Treaty of Rome was overwhelmingly trade-oriented, its
primary aim being to create a Common Market. It set up a customs
union and common customs tariff and a common agricultural
policy, as well as provisions for the free movement of persons,
services and capital. It provided rules regarding competition and the
harmonization of measures affecting "the establishment or
functioning of the Common Market". It established the European
Investment Bank, its task being "to contribute ... to the balanced

and steady development of the Common Market in the interest of the Community". It set up the European Assembly (not changed to "Parliament" until 1987) consisting of delegates designated by each Member State, with "advisory and supervisory powers" only. It also had provisions for creating and setting up the Council, the Commission, the Court of Justice, the budget and the first financial year, and the starting time-scales for all the Community institutions.

It should be clearly understood that an inchoate federal union was initiated by the Treaty of Rome itself. This becomes apparent on considering the respective powers and duties of the Commission, the Council and the Court of Justice. For example, if the Commission considers that a Member State has failed to observe the Treaty, the Commission can take it to the Court which, if it finds accordingly, can impose **penalties** on the Member State. To make the UK's subordination clear, in the Act ratifying our Accession to the Treaty, the European Communities Act 1973, clause 2, laid down that Community law should prevail over English and Scottish law and, **without further enactment**, should be recognized in law, and be "enforced, allowed and followed accordingly". Only a matter of months before, the Heath White Paper of July 1971 had misleadingly and dishonestly said: "The common law will remain the basis of our legal system, and our courts will continue to operate as they do at present".

The Preamble to the Treaty of Rome referred to "the foundations of an ever closer union", "a common commercial policy", and the decision "to create a European Economic Community". Outwardly for the world at large, the Common Market was the sole intention, but the secret agenda for the founding fathers and the inner circle of the original Six, (France, Germany, Italy, Netherlands, Belgium and Luxembourg) was integration to eventual federal union. This theme was taken forward in subsequent Treaties, for instance, Article 1 of the **Maastricht Treaty** states: "This Treaty marks a **new stage in the process of creating an ever closer union**...". Also, the Maastricht Preamble speaks of "a new stage in the process of

European integration...", and, for good measure, continuing "the process of creating an ever closer Union", "...in order to advance European integration".

The Single European Act 1986 (SEA) was the next major Treaty in the series. Margaret Thatcher subsequently admitted that it had been a mistake to go along with this Act and claimed that she was deceived into accepting it. It seems that the Foreign Office stressed to her the Act's advantages in improving the internal market whilst ignoring or minimizing the further erosion of national sovereignty and the Act's provisions facilitating progress towards integration and federal union. Lord Beloff (see his excellent book *Britain and European Union, Dialogue of the Deaf)* quotes from Thatcher's Memoirs: "The Single European Act, contrary to my intentions and my understanding of the formal undertakings given at the time, had provided new scope for the European Commission and the European Court to press forward in the direction of centralization". The Act provided for establishing the internal market by the end of 1992, and for introducing "common measures" on police cooperation, visas, extradition and immigration. The Act's Preamble referred to monetary union as a Community goal to be "progressively realized", although not among the 1992 priorities. There were provisions for the environment, for research and technological development and for better use of the structural funds or regional funds of the "Cohesion" policy for reducing disparities between richer and poorer regions of the Community. The Assembly, transformed into the European Parliament, was given increased power enabling it to amend legislation and in some cases to have the final say. The Act also provided for cooperation in the sphere of foreign policy by consultation leading to convergence and the implementation of joint action. Further, it called for closer cooperation on European security, though so as not to conflict with NATO or the WEU. Of significant importance, in a dozen or more cases the veto was ceded to qualified majority voting, thus giving away the UK's strong negotiating position in the areas concerned.

The intention to go forward on the federal trail had been reiterated in the **Declaration on European Union** in the Stuttgart Summit in June 1983, and the SEA helped that process along. Geoffrey Howe, Foreign Secretary at the time, admitted that because the Declaration was not legally binding, they attached less significance than they should have done to this blueprint for the future — another example of Government turning a blind eye to yet a further item added to the quantities of evidence of developing federalism. The Single European Act had been nurtured by the French socialist Jacques Delors on his becoming President of the Commission in 1985, and over the following years, with Delors' stimulus, the French-German axis refocused its drive for progress. In addressing the Parliament in 1988/89 Delors outlined integrationist policies including his aim for restructured Community institutions whereby the Parliament would be the Community's House of Representatives, the Council of Ministers would be the Senate, and the Commission would be the Executive Government. Following the ambush of the UK at the Rome Summit meeting in October 1990, Margaret Thatcher resigned as Prime Minister after being undermined by Geoffrey Howe and others in her Cabinet. This result was an objective of her arch-adversary Delors and facilitated the progress of the next stage in the Long March towards federalism, the **Maastricht Treaty** of 1992. The Single European Act and the Maastricht Treaty were both regarded by Lord Beloff as "major British diplomatic defeats", though in the usual way within the UK they were acclaimed as successes. What is clear is that in Maastricht the federal ratchet clicked on several stages. The Preamble, as mentioned, intoned the mantra of "ever closer union", and outlined the plan. The powers of the Community institutions were extended in various ways. This Treaty of 7 Titles, 17 Protocols and 33 Declarations established a European Union, (Article A), and citizenship of the Union (Article B), whereby every citizen of the Union living in a Member State other than his own may vote and stand as a candidate in municipal elections and also in elections for the European Parliament. Stated objectives in Article B were:

- strengthening cohesion through economic and monetary union;

- implementing common foreign and security policies, leading to common defence;

- close cooperation on justice and home affairs;
- maintaining in full and building on the acquis communautaire.

Article C laid down that the Union is to be "served by a single institutional framework". This may well be code for a Constitution, and become one of the Community's mantras in ensuing Treaties, like "ever closer union", so that in the months and years ahead the Community can say that a federal union and a Constitution, are what was meant all along. Article C also requires "consistency" in external relations, security, economic and development policies, for which the Council and the Commission are responsible. "Consistency" looks like a weasel word half way towards "harmonization". Article D formed the European Council comprising the Heads of State or of Government of the Member States, assisted by their Foreign Ministers, and the President of the Commission, assisted by a Member of the Commission. The European Council's task is to define the general political guidelines and impetus for development of the Community. Article F requires the Community to respect fundamental rights under the **European Convention on Human Rights** of 1950, as general principles of Community law.

The core of this Treaty is the section on **Economic and Monetary Policy** (Articles 102-109 and Protocols), where Delors' three-stage plan, the convergence criteria and the European Central Bank arrangements are spelt out.

Article J provides that the European Council shall define the principles of and general guidelines for the common foreign and security policy, and that Member States shall ensure that their national policies **conform** to the common positions; and that the Commission shall be fully associated with this work.

Article K provides for cooperation in the fields of Justice and Home Affairs, and Member States must regard as matters of common interest many areas including: asylum and immigration policies, drug addiction, international fraud, customs, police and judicial, civil and criminal matters. Again, the Commission is to be fully associated with this work.

Article N provides that any Member State **or the Commission** may submit proposals for the amendment of the Treaties; and that a Conference of Member States shall take place in 1996 for revision of this Treaty. The "competence" of the **Commission** is extended in various areas including: Economic and Monetary Policy, Education, Culture, Public Health, Consumer Protection, Trans-European networks, Industry, Development Cooperation, Economic and Social Cohesion, and Environment.

The European Parliament's powers are increased whereby it can veto and propose amendments to Community Acts, and it can dismiss the Commission (Article 144).

At the Maastricht Summit in December 1991, the UK was as usual isolated on almost every subject and regarded as "obstructionist and intransigent", but they managed to have the words **"with a federal goal"**. removed from the Treaty, after a lot of wrangling. Here again, for the wilful unbelievers and concealers in the UK Government and Establishment, was hard evidence of the federal intention. Nevertheless, in the Final Act of the Treaty the words: "...with a view to the achievement of **political union...**" are spelt out.

It is worth pointing out that both Brussels and London are reluctant to publicize and make available copies of the Treaties. After Maastricht was agreed, in Denmark 500,000 copies were distributed without delay, whereas by contrast in the UK HMSO (now the Stationery Office) distributed copies to MPs, but the

public were side-lined. Eventually, an independent Oxford publisher produced the text which, out of indignation at official silence and delay, he called *The Unseen Treaty*. Also, another independent enterprise, the **British Management Data Foundation** produced a well put-together and annotated text.

Every Treaty takes the **process** of federalisation forward and prepares the ground for the next in the series. After having launched and piloted Maastricht through, Jacques Delors' Commission Presidency (1985-95) still had 2 or 3 years to run, and he was thus able to guide and give impetus to the follow-on **Amsterdam Treaty**.

The **Amsterdam Treaty** Draft was agreed in June 1997, the Treaty was signed in October 1997, and it entered into force in May 1999. I received my copy of the Treaty in November 1997 — some 590 pages, and much heavier reading than even that figure implies — and it comprises 8 Titles, 34 Protocols, 51 adopted Declarations and 8 noted Declarations. The labyrinthine method adopted by the Community for its Treaties is that each Treaty does not replace but amends each of the preceding Treaties and also, as it were, has a life of its own. So the full document I received from the Foreign Office contained some 290 pages of amendments and additions to the Treaties of the European Coal and Steel Community (ECSC), of the European Atomic Energy Community (EAEC), of Rome (as amended by the Single European Act), and of Maastricht. Then the Treaty of Amsterdam **attached** the Consolidated Treaties of Rome and Maastricht (a further 300 pages) "as they result from the amendments". Amsterdam strangely described these attachments as being "for illustrative purposes", as if they may not be used for general interpretation. So after all this, the result in basic terms is: the Treaty of Amsterdam, shorn of its amendments, remains as a shell or administrative skeleton, and the operative matters are contained in the new version of the Treaty on European Union which is split into two re-numbered parts comprising the Consolidated Maastricht Treaty and the Consolidated Rome Treaty, both parts including the Amsterdam amendments.

In addition to this tortuous system of Treaty amendment, the Community drafting is so verbose and convoluted, the cross-referencing so numerous, the text re-grouping and Article re-numbering so confusing, and the many definitions are so loose and imprecise, that one is forced to realize that this bureaucratic written nightmare is constructed in this manner specifically to confuse the outer world and to allow the Commission and other Community institutions a free hand in interpretation and action. For example, there has clearly been much fudging and breach by several Member States of the Maastricht Convergence Criteria (Articles 109j, 104c and Protocols) providing the standards for entry into the single currency, which demonstrates that the Treaty is open to any distortion in the hands of the Commission and colluding Member States. This fudging is made easier because the statistics to be used in this connection are provided by the Commission itself (Article 5 of the Protocol on the Convergence Criteria). Who will guard the guards themselves?

Happily, the **British Management Data Foundation** has again produced an excellent book (a mere 350 pages) comprising the text of the Treaties and detailed notes and a three-column table of comparisons, achieving as much success as is possible in getting order out of such unpromising material.

The inchoate federal nature of the Treaty of Rome was discernible from the beginning, and this tendency was taken forward by the Single European Act, and continued in Maastricht and then Amsterdam. This trend is evidenced at each stage by the increasing importance being given to the Community institutions. Their growing power is being created indirectly by the extension of qualified majority voting and by progressive harmonization of laws, and directly by provisions in the Treaties, to the point where the Community institutions are gradually predominating over the Member States.

The powers of **the European Council** have been extended by Amsterdam in several areas: in cases of breach by a Member State of fundamental principles of liberty, democracy, human rights and the rule of law, where that State may lose certain rights, including voting rights (Articles 6 and 7, Title 1); also under provisions concerning Closer Cooperation or "Flexibility", employment, foreign and security policy, and police and judicial cooperation. **The Council of Ministers'** role is generally to coordinate the economic policies of the Member States. The broad intention is that qualified majority voting (QMV) will become the normal procedure, to avoid the use of the veto frustrating the wishes of 14 Member States, especially as on enlargement it will become impossible in practical terms to retain the veto. Amsterdam extended QMV into a dozen or more new areas. The Council will increase cooperation between Member States regarding non-discrimination, the movement of persons, asylum, immigration and border control, and the Schengen acquis (the Agreements signed in 1985-1996) is being introduced into the Treaty itself. The UK and Ireland are not parties to the Schengen border arrangements. The UK having agreed to sign the "Social Chapter" at Amsterdam, its Protocol has been repealed and the Social Chapter provisions incorporated in the main body of the Treaty. In the field of Common Foreign and Security Policy, the provisions have been redrafted and expanded so that the Community will take the lead in formulating and guiding policy and making sure that Member States' policies conform to those of the Community. Amsterdam has extended the role of the **European Parliament** and its involvement in the legislative process, by the principle of **co-decision** (under Article 251) whereby it will act on an equal footing with the Council in a wide number of new areas. The EP's activities have been widened into areas where it may **endorse** actions of the Council; into the **consultation** procedure where the Council will take into account the EP's opinion; and into the **cooperation** procedure where the Council must take into account the EP's opinion and proposed amendments before voting on the action. The EP has also acquired the right and duty to approve the appointment of the President of the

Commission (Article 214). The power of the **Commission** has not greatly been increased in specific or direct ways in Amsterdam, except that Article 219 now requires it to work under the **political** guidance of its President. It will be interesting to see what effect this may have on its performance. Indirectly, however, the power of the Commission is growing all the time, because as the guardian of the Treaties and initiator of all legislative proposals, whenever the interests and "competences" of the Community are widened by Treaty provisions, by enlargement or by Member States surrendering vetoes, exclusions and options, the ambit of the Commission is inevitably extended. **The Court of Justice's** jurisdiction has been widened so it may give preliminary rulings on the validity of framework decisions and review the legality of actions by Member States and the Community (Article 35, Title VI). The powers of the **Court of Auditors** have not been extended in executive terms, and may have been circumscribed by a new provision whereby its right of access to information from the European Investment Bank is subject to agreement with the Commission (Article 248). As the Commission is widely connected with the disbursement of funds from the EU budget, it seems strange that it should have any influence on the Court of Auditors' right of access to information concerning budget funds. On various occasions over the years the Court of Auditors' Report has exposed defalcations, mismanagement and misappropriation of budget funds on a massive scale, but the Treaties give them no teeth, and scandalously the other Community institutions have never done anything to improve the position.

Although the single currency was not directly covered in the debates on Amsterdam, the Stability Pact was discussed and agreed. In essence, this Pact requires that States which have joined the single currency and have been deemed to have met the convergence criteria for doing so, must continue to keep their economies within the necessary criteria levels. Amsterdam also established the basic principles of the new Exchange Rate Mechanism for those States not joining the single currency. Both these matters were contained in Resolutions of the European Council and attached to the Treaty. I will revert to the Stability Pact and the new ERM later on.

A Declaration attached to the Treaty speaks of the growing importance of the **Western European Union** (WEU) its possible eventual integration into the EU, and the intention to foster closer links with the WEU.

There were also new Articles concerning social protection of workers (Article 137) and equal opportunities and equal treatment in the field of employment (Article 141), and "the prevention of and fight against fraud" (Article 280).

The Article on **Subsidiarity and Proportionality** (Article 5) has not been amended, but Amsterdam attached a Protocol on the subject. **Subsidiarity** means broadly that the Community will take action only if and insofar as the objectives of the proposed action cannot be sufficiently achieved by the Member States. **Proportionality** means that any action by the Community shall not go beyond what is necessary to achieve the objectives of the Treaty. Article 5 has always been regarded as an **illusory benefit** and the merest lip-service to independent national action and even as a token has been constantly ignored by the Community institutions, specially the Commission. It is regarded as legally unenforceable. The Protocol indicates the limited nature of the principle of Article 5 by stating that it shall respect the general provisions and the objectives of the Treaty, particularly as regards the maintaining in full of the acquis communautaire, and it shall not affect the principles developed by the Court of Justice regarding the relationship between national and Community law. Purported improvements have been made in the field of **Transparency**, to the end that decisions of Community institutions shall be taken as openly as possible. Under Article 207 the Council is to facilitate greater access to legislative documents; and under the Protocol on the Role of National Parliaments in the EU, the Commission is required to provide prompt availability of the relevant documents "in good time" to national parliaments. The facilities under these two Articles have been notoriously absent or underprovided in the past, and great improvement is much overdue.

After Amsterdam was signed in October 1997, the Parliament passed a Resolution, appended to the Treaty, in the usual florid high-flown style proclaiming the need for a "much greater role" for the Parliament in future Treaty amendments, and for more and more integration. Its overall evaluation of Amsterdam was that it **"makes a further step on the unfinished path towards the construction of a European political union"**.

I do not see the Nice Treaty being the final one. It is likely to be "more of the same", in the sense that it will surely give greater and wider powers to the Community institutions at the expense of the Member States, and particularly to the Commission, the Parliament and the Council, thus getting ever closer to the concept of Delors, of the Commission as the Executive Government, with the Parliament and the Council being the House of Representatives and the Senate.

Chapter Four

ECONOMIC AND MONETARY UNION
(THE TROJAN HORSE)

*The debate in the UK has always underestimated the
momentum behind Economic and Monetary Union*
Yves-Thibault de Silguy, French Commissioner
for Monetary Union, November 1998

*A European currency will lead to member nations transferring
their sovereignty over financial and wage policies as well as
in monetary affairs. It is an illusion to think that States can
hold onto their autonomy over taxation policies*
Hans Tietmeyer, President of the Bundesbank

*Tax co-ordination is now an ordinary, though difficult, subject
which has a permanent place on the EU Agenda*
Mario Monti, Italian Commissioner for financial
integration and taxation, September 1998

...fiscal consolidation needs to be pushed forward more aggressively
Wim Duisenberg, Dutch President of the
European Central Bank, August 1998

*The permanent fixing of exchange rates would deprive individual countries
of an important instrument for the correction of economic imbalance*
The Delors Report of the Committee for the study of EMU, 1989

*Economic and Monetary Union is,
in the final analysis, a political project*
John Bruton, former Prime Minister of Ireland

*The primary target of a monetary union — as well as the whole history
of the European Community — is a political one*
Helmut Schlesinger, former Bundesbank President, 1995

Why was the single currency ever thought of? The ostensible reason
was that it was required for the Single Market, but the Governor of
the Bank of England, Eddie George has said that he does "not think
it is necessary, in any kind of sense". Likewise a fixed exchange rate
system is not necessary. The North Atlantic Free Trade Area
(NAFTA) between the USA, Canada, Mexico and potentially other
countries operates successfully without the constraints of any such
onerous machinery. In fact, the whole paraphernalia of EMU, that
flightless creature, is an extremely expensive charade of economics
camouflaging a one-way street to political union. And embedding
the Member States in the Procrustean EMU will continue to be a
painful business.

All the continental Member States view EMU as a burdensome
and expensive but necessary stage in the progress along the path
towards federal union, their shared political goal of binding in
Germany to preserve peace. They all know full well how
burdensome it is, because each Member State has been obliged to
wrench and distort its economy in order to comply, after a fashion,
with Maastricht Convergence Criteria (MCC). I say "after a
fashion", because several of the States have not in reality qualified
on a proper interpretation of the Articles of the Treaty, but have
been allowed into the net, partly because of the elasticity of the
wording of the Treaty and partly through the complaisance of the
Commission. Even at the outset, several States were in breach of the
MCC limit of **gross debt** of 60% of Gross Domestic Product
(GDP), including Spain, Germany and Portugal, with Belgium and
Italy having gross debt figures of 122% and 121% respectively, over
double the limit. Regarding the criteria for **budget deficits**, the limit
being 3% of GDP, throughout 1992 to 1996, France, Belgium, Italy,
Finland, Portugal, and Austria were all over the limit, some

considerably so, though by Euro-day they had more or less managed by belt-tightening contrivances, fiddling and creative accounting to be allowed to enter the Single Currency. Those are not good portents for a stable and effective future for EMU, and the prospects for the Treaty requirement of **sustainability**, after all the financial antics even to reach the starting gate, are very poor. Over the first six months of life the Euro declined by some 10% against the pound sterling and 14% against the US dollar, and in late June 1999, Romano Prodi the new President of the Commission and former Italian Prime Minister was wondering out loud whether Italy would be able in the longer term to remain in the Single Currency.

Meanwhile, alone out of all the Member States, the UK Government's approach is to attempt to conceal or ignore the existence of the real continental objective and the true nature of the Single Currency/EMU as a Trojan horse. They seek to treat the Single Currency as a purely economic matter and have produced five economic tests by which to judge it, and express a clear intention and desire to join the Single Currency as soon as they deem it practicable. The serious setback for Labour in the Euro-elections in early June 1999 has diluted the strength and urgency of their drive towards the Single Currency, for the moment, but not the general course of their policy. An all-party Early Day Motion put down by six MPs is in terms "That this House calls on Her Majesty's Government to publish a White Paper on the **constitutional, economic and political implications** of the United Kingdom joining the European Single Currency". This Motion (EDM 185) has been signed by over 100 MPs, but so far there is no sign of a White Paper, and the Government are steadfastly refusing to give any response on the political and constitutional implications.

There have been monetary unions in the past, though none worked for long, and they broke down because of fiscal disparities or asymmetric shocks in the economy of their Members, lacking as they did political union. The Austro-German Monetary Union between Austria and the German States, which lasted for 10 years from 1857; although it continued for the German States which became politically united in 1871 under Bismarck. The Latin Monetary Union of 1865 between France, Belgium, Switzerland, Italy and Greece, and the Scandinavian Monetary Union of 1873 between Sweden, Denmark and Norway, both lasted for a while, but lacking political unity their fiscal and economic differences led to the breakdown of the system. In 1979, the notorious Exchange Rate Mechanism (ERM) was created. The UK was initially sceptical, but in 1987 it started to shadow the deutschmark and joined in October 1990. Our two-year period in the ERM was an unmitigated and extremely expensive disaster. It provoked the UK's worst recession in over half a century. Period for period, more businesses went bankrupt than ever before (three times more than in 1989, the year before entry into the ERM), over 60,000 homes were repossessed in each year, 1.75 million homes suffered "negative equity" whereby the property value fell below its mortgage, and unemployment nearly doubled. Entry was **a dangerous leap in the dark**, and unbelievably neither our previous Government nor our present one seem to have learnt anything from it. In October 1992 the UK and Italy had to leave the ERM, unable to sustain the required levels, and by August 1993, amid turmoil and recrimination the ERM collapsed, with the permitted bands widened to a meaningless plus or minus 15%. The clearest message of **cause and effect** is that during the span of ERM, continental Member States fell into deep recession with greatly increasing unemployment, whereas by contrast the UK (except for its reckless escapade in the ERM) flourished and had diminishing unemployment.

It seems clear that each country, an intricate entity composed of many different attributes and subject to diverse influences, must retain the greatest flexibility of action to respond to a wide range of economic impacts, external shocks and influences. Two of the foremost tools are control of exchange rates and interest rates, and these are denied to any Member of EMU. Further, the **Stability Pact**, the subject of a European Council Resolution incorporated in the Treaty, provides that a Member State in breach of the criteria of budget deficit of 3% of GDP or Government debt of 60%, would be subject, within a limited time-frame, to the imposition of monetary deposits turning into **fines**. The ceilings of these possible fines are, regarding a deficit breach, 0.5% of GDP, and for a debt breach, 2% of GDP. So the maximum penalties for the UK would be of the order of £3.5 billion and £14 billion respectively. The logic of even contemplating the application of fines of this magnitude for countries that have found it impossible to meet the required financial criteria escapes me. There are already Member States in breach of the Stability Pact, but there are indications that the penalties will not be imposed. So much for the Treaty when it does not suit events.

It simply does not make sense for the "one-size-must-fit-all" straitjacket of EMU to be capable of being successfully applied and operated by 15 States all with different economic cycles and fiscal parities. There is no such thing as a correct exchange rate for the EU. As long as economies diverge, no exchange rate will be permanently right. The UK, so different from the other 14 States in many ways, also has a divergent economic cycle. Of recent times, it has had an 8-to-9-year cycle, being in deficit in the 1980-1 recession and in surplus in the 1988-9 boom. For most of our time as a Member of the Community our economic cycle has diverged from most of the EU, and that divergence is growing. At the same time our cycle has been more similar to that of the USA. Wrong but unavoidable fixed interest rates would cause exaggerated conditions, either excessive boom or prolonged downturn. The fact is that the UK economy is structurally different from the rest of the EU, and joining the EMU would increase those differences and destabilize our economy. Some of these **main differences** are:-

(a)   Tax levels. Both our basic and higher rates of personal tax are the lowest in the EU. Our business taxes are lower than the majority of Member States. These taxes as well as higher rate threshold levels, wealth tax (where relevant), and social security payments all vary considerably from country to country.

(b) The liability for pensions. This is one of the greatest dangers in the EU structure. UK pensions are to a large extent funded, whereas pensions in most of the other States are unfunded. An indication of the seriousness of this position is that the UK's liability for unfunded pensions is 7% of GDP, in contrast to France's of 118% of GDP, Germany's of 115% of GDP and Italy's 78% of GDP. These figures are staggering and dangerous, and I will return to this problem.

(c) Our non-wage labour costs are lower than in the majority of other States.

(d) Our unemployment level is of recent years markedly lower than in most of the other States.

(e) A higher percentage of homes are owned here than in many other States, and mortgage debt is a much bigger proportion of GDP here than in the rest of the EU.

(f) In the UK personal investment in equities is a higher proportion than in other States, and corporate finance here is mainly through equity, in contrast to continental businesses which tend to use bank loans.

(g) The UK has a lower proportion of total trade in the EU (around 46%) than the other States.

(h) The UK has a much greater amount of overseas investment beyond the EU than other States.

(i) The UK has by far the most important investment and banking centre in the EU, much greater than all the other States.

(j) The UK is the only oil exporter in the EU.

All these differences, and others, make the UK much more different from the other 14 States than they are amongst themselves.

Since the start of the single currency at the beginning of 1999 with 11 participants, with the UK, Denmark and Sweden remaining free, there is an increasing impetus in the Commission towards further tax harmonization, to curb what it regards as "harmful tax competition". In the second half of 1998 Austria, which then held the Presidency, put common taxation high on the agenda, and since then the Parliament (EP) has called for a European income tax to be directly levied on EU citizens — all of us. Tax harmonization which, there is little doubt, will gradually be introduced, will be extremely damaging and onerous to the UK. This is apparent because most of its taxes are at lower levels than amongst the other States, and so harmonization would obviously be upwards. To begin with, the Commission has stated that EMU will require greater "fiscal disbursements". Indeed, the MacDougall Report, the Commission's study into the economies of the EMU, said that the EMU would require a **minimum** of 5 to 7% of GDP to be made available to Brussels, in contrast to the present ceiling of 1.27%. If implemented, this would require annual contributions by States to the EU Budget some **five times greater** than present levels. The biggest current threat is the withholding tax of 20% on investment interest. This would be a devastating blow to the City, and might lead to thousands of job-losses and billions of investment being emigrated to other centres such as New York, Tokyo or Zurich. It should be remembered that the City acquired a large part of this business precisely as a result of New York imposing a similar sort of tax in the first place, causing emigration of funds to the City of London. Meanwhile, harmonization of indirect taxes, specially VAT, will continue. Our zero-rated essentials like food, childrens clothing, books, newspapers, new houses, rail, air and bus travel are not sacrosanct and at some stage may be forced to yield, costing us further billions. Most of the other Member States have VAT in various percentages on all these items.

Various polls show that the majority of the British people wish to keep the pound and to reject the euro, and that a substantial and increasing minority (some 46% at the last count) wish to leave the EU altogether. In spite of this evidence, the Government maintains its desire to join the euro. Sadly, the same tired old arguments from the same tired old stagers — Howe, Heseltine, Clarke — support the single currency, and as apologists for the ERM try unconvincingly to argue that the devastation of the 1990-92 black hole while in the ERM was not caused by the ERM itself. Leaving that aside, a **new ERM** was formed at the beginning of 1999 to act as a framework for States not participating in the euro. This new ERM was established in a Resolution of the European Council agreed in June 1997 at Amsterdam and incorporated in the Treaty. Participation is voluntary (see Resolution, paragraph 1.6), but once a State decides it wishes to join the single currency, it has to join the new ERM first. For any non-euro area State which joins the new ERM, a central rate against the euro will be defined, with a standard fluctuation band of plus or minus 15%.

The cost of meeting the Maastricht convergence criteria all round the EU is conveniently forgotten, ignored or swept under the carpet. Studies have been carried out on the subject, and one shows that to ensure that the UK budget deficit remains below the required 3% of GDP at the bottom of a recession would involve tax increases or public spending cuts in the region of between £28 billion and £46 billion. Another study showed that meeting the deficit and debt criteria would reduce the GDP of all Member States by an average of 2.6%, with the heavily indebted States — Italy, Belgium and Greece — suffering a GDP reduction of 6%. A Danish Study forecast that over 10 million **more** people would lose their jobs because of meeting the criteria, and an UNCTAD (United Nations Conference on Trade and Development) Report calculated that full implementation of the criteria would increase EU unemployment to 15%. It is clear that the vaunted transaction cost savings through the single currency will be paltry compared with the cost even of the transition into the EMU.

Over the whole EMU structure, rules the unelected, unaccountable European Central Bank (ECB) under its Dutch President Wim Duisenberg, set up under Article 105 and Protocol

No. 18 of the Treaty. It operates within the European System of Central Banks (ESCB) with its basic tasks: to define and implement the EU's monetary policy, to conduct foreign exchange operations, and to hold, manage and use the official foreign reserves of Member States up to ECU 50 billion (of the order of £30 billion), with the power to call for further foreign reserve assets. Its stated "primary objective" is to "maintain price stability", apparently regardless of the stringent needs of some or most of the States for higher, or lower, interest and exchange rates. The irony of the "one-size-must-fit-all" regime is that it may fit some States some times, and other States at other times, but it will **never** fit any one state all the time, and **never** fit all the States at any one time, far less all the time. So this means that a number, maybe a majority, of States will be for most of the time in conditions of economic stringency and disarray, with the resulting disorder for jobs, homes and businesses.

All 15 Member States diverge widely from each other in many ways, and EMU will exacerbate those divergences. The main economic differences of the UK I have mentioned are all substantial and important and some of them are real danger points if our Government jeopardizes, or rather condemns, the whole future of the UK by joining the single currency. **Joining the EMU would be a re-run of our 1990-92 ERM debacle, and worse, because there is worse to come in the EU, and because joining is stated in the Treaty to be "irrevocable".**

Chapter Five

EU INSTITUTIONS

Today's enemy is bureaucracy, and the people are losing the struggle
Vaclav Klaus, Prime Minister of the Czech Republic, 1995

The greater the power, the more dangerous the abuse
Edmund Burke, 1771

Big Brother is watching you
George Orwell, *1984*

They are grown used to their own unreason; chaos is their cosmos
G.K. Chesterton's Essay *The Mad Official*

I recall one low point when nine Foreign Ministers solemnly assembled in Brussels to spend several hours discussing how to resolve our differences on standardising a fixed position of rear-view mirrors on agricultural tractors
Memoirs of James Callaghan, former Prime Minister, 1987

Laws which are passed for a large area lose their vigour, and such a soulless despotism ... ultimately collapses into anarchy
Immanuel Kant

The Commission

It should have been realized long since that the Commission is not a civil service as conventionally understood in a democratic nation. It is more and more an **Executive Government**, which is how it regards itself, with a built-in civil service. This outcome, though of much earlier origins, was central to Jacques Delors' plans throughout his Presidency of the Commission from 1985 to 1995.

During his tenure, he packed the Commission with French Socialists, so that it should run the EU for France. In 1991 Delors said that the EU must become a super-state and a military superpower. A central strand of the Commission's power is that from the beginning it has been the sole source having the right to **initiate** legislation. Theo Waigel, former German Finance Minister and others have called for this monopoly to be ended. (In passing, it is interesting to note that the Commission's primary powers — Article 211 of the Treaty — are circumscribed by the words: "In order to ensure the proper functioning and development of the **common market**, the Commission shall...". But this limitation is ignored by the Commission and goes unchallenged. This is another example of the Treaty meaning what the EU institutions want it to mean). The Treaty under Articles 133 and 300 already gives the Commission the power and duty to conduct negotiations with foreign countries and international organizations such as WTO, and the Commission is constantly seeking, with regular success, to extend its influence and its right to be consulted in all new developments under the Treaty. It still, without any regard for "subsidiarity" vigorously pumps out great quantities of legislation in its own esoteric jargon adding to the EU's "acquis communautaire". Of recent years, there is a greater volume of Commission **Regulations**, (as opposed to Directives), because they become immediately binding and are produced by Committees of **officials**, without the need for any involvement by elected politicians. The Commission has over the years arranged for the funding of the European Movement, a pro-EU propaganda operation, also funded from the Foreign Office and the USA, and that Movement and the Foreign Office's Information Research Department (IRD) have had long-standing programmes of unpublicized but repeated briefings to persuade people of influence to the EU cause.

But on the contrary, it is vitally important that the British people as a whole be alerted and understand the extent to which we are **already** almost in a federal union. Our present position, which is by no means new, is that we are under the domination of a centralized dirigiste, quasi-totalitarian bureaucracy, unelected and under no day-to-day supervision or control. Our Parliament can only pass legislation which accords with the Treaty and the Commission's Directives and Regulations (of which there were over 23,000 not so long ago); our Supreme Court, no longer supreme, is subject to the European Court; every company and business in the country has to conform to an enormous range of far-reaching but often pettifogging regulations from the Commission, as a result of which thousands of businesses have been bankrupted; company mergers and takeovers cannot take place without the approval of the EU Competition Commission — for instance, at the end of June 1999 the Belgian Commissioner for Competition Karel Van Miert was scrutinizing the BMW/Rover deal; some duties and taxes (e.g. VAT) have been harmonized for some time, and a widespread range of further tax harmonization is on the stocks. A country with all those restraints cannot claim to be free and sovereign.

The fact that such a dirigiste oligarchy as the Commission is prone to corruption and fraud should not come as a surprise, and so it proved. At the beginning of 1999, five Commissioners, including the French Edith Cresson and the Spaniard Manuel Marin, as well as the Luxembourg President Jacques Santer were challenged by the Parliament (EP), but then the latter lost its nerve and backed down. However, in March the EP took courage and invoked its power under Article 201 to censure the Commission, whereby all Commissioners are required to resign as a body. Strangely, the Article provides that they stay in office until replaced by the governments of Member States, under Article 214, which took place in the autumn of 1999. By that Article, a new rule requires that the new President must be approved by the EP, and that the new President shall agree the new Commissioners with the governments of the Member States. These are new powers for the EP and the President of the Commission. The censured President Jacques Santer left office and Romano Prodi, former Prime Minister of Italy who like a number of his predecessors has been the subject of criminal investigation, has been appointed President, with the support of Tony Blair. Barely in office, Prodi made strong statements in support of the drive towards federal union and for the need for tax harmonization as an integral part of EMU. Whether Prodi is the best man for the job is almost academic, because so much in the EU is decided on the "Buggins' turn" principle. Small country, then big country; Northern country, then Southern country; one major party, then another; and so on. Whether a better man/woman is available for a particular job is secondary to "Buggins' turn". Another new rule, in Article 219, requires the Commission to "work under the political guidance of its President". It is not clear what the implications and ramifications of this new rule are, but it smacks unpleasantly of the old Soviet regime.

It is within the Commission's ambit of authority to draft the **EU Budget** each year, and consideration and debate of it by the Council is regularly a task involving great tension, dispute and ill feeling between the States. The hard-won UK rebate won by Margaret Thatcher is increasingly challenged and under threat, and it seems likely that it will be removed or reduced, as ever by some compromise, in the next year or two. In 1999, Germany, who believes it pays too big a share, was going to fight vigorously for a reduction, but, again probably by way of some compromise, did not greatly protest. It seems likely that the overall ceiling of the Budget will have to be raised substantially in the foreseeable future, and that will of course give rise to really major horse-trading, rows and infighting between the Member States.

We should not lose sight of the **Corpus Juris** project prepared by the Commission in 1997 and presented to the Association of European Jurists. It is intended to set up a system with a European Public Prosecutor with wide powers and overriding jurisdiction in and over all Member States. This would introduce the Inquisitional system of justice whereby the investigating prosecutor is a judge. The European Public Prosecutor would have a delegate in each

State, and a Euro-warrant for arrest would be valid across the whole of the EU. The system would include "coercive measures" including detention for up to 6 or 9 months pending investigation. This system would subordinate national law throughout the EU and would destroy the English safeguards of habeas corpus and trial by jury, which have been bulwarks of our legal system for centuries, and would be an important step towards a complete, federal European system of criminal law based on Roman law and Napoleonic law. Such a system would be completely alien to the UK and Ireland, but quite familiar to all the continental States, whose laws have a similar base. If the UK remains in the EU, the English legal system of a thousand years will be in serious jeopardy.

Looking yet again through the Treaties, it is difficult to see any area of EU activity where the Commission is **not** either taking the prime role of inter-State negotiations, legislating by Regulations, decision-making or implementing and enforcing decisions, or at least playing a leading part by making a proposal or giving its opinion and guidance or being consulted. The Commission truly is the Executive Government of the EU, and very little happens without its say-so.

The European Parliament

But far more numerous was the herd of such,
Who think too little and who talk too much
John Dryden

Each Treaty progressively strengthens the range and powers of the Commission and the Parliament, so as to approach nearer and nearer to the well-established plan fostered by Jacques Delors for the EU Government to be the Commission as the Executive body, with the Parliament as the legislature (or House of Commons) and the Council as the Senate. Under the Amsterdam Treaty there are provisions involving the EP in more co-decision, consultation and cooperation. At present the UK has 87 MEPs, out of a total of 626. Article 189 contains a new rule that the maximum number is now 700, so when the EU enlarges, each State will have to reduce its representation. As I mentioned earlier, in March 1999, the EP flexed its muscles and sacked all the Commissioners, and that power is in effect the only restraint upon the Commission. It is also being considered whether the EP should have more flexibility and be permitted to sack one or more Commissioners, rather than just all of them en bloc.

I referred earlier to the **Draft Constitution** contained in a working paper produced by a Committee of the EP in 1993. Incidentally, this Draft included a provision for a Member State to leave the EU and be accorded **"preferential associate status"**. I am not aware of any other document emanating from the EU or its institutions which provides for or makes reference to a Member State leaving the EU. I telephoned the UK EP Office in London in June 1999, and they told me that the 1993 Draft was not pursued. However, there may well be further work going on covertly in some part of the Commission on the preparation of a Draft Constitution, which has been called for in recent times in some Member States and which is on the agenda of the long-term federal plan.

The EU elections in June 1999 were a boost for the UK Conservatives, but their increased numbers, which doubled to 36, raised again the question of which European Group they should be affiliated to. This is always a problem because nearly all the other States are either Socialist/Communist or left of centre. The European Peoples Party (EPP) now the biggest group and allegedly right of centre, is the least dissimilar, but its stated objectives are the single currency and integration towards a federal form of Union. This difficulty points up the UK's isolation in a swarm of integrationists. William Hague and his MEPs are trying to find a formula with which to negotiate a continuing link with the EPP which does not bind the UK Conservative MEPs to the federalist aspects of EPP policy. It is thought that an on-going connection with the EPP would assist the enlarged UK Tory group to have a better chance of influencing the agenda of the new EP's business through gaining in the allocation of Committee chairmanships and places on delegations.

Although it was the EP's exercise of its Treaty power that removed all the Commissioners in March 1999, the MEPs themselves are by no means free from taint or criticism for fraud and fiddling. They have a wide range of excessive expenses allowances which are regularly abused and which, taken with their salaries, raise the total income from EP service to around £200,000 annually for many MEPs. Various expenses including for sessions attendance, travel, accommodation, research and secretarial assistants, are claimed and go through on the nod, without having to be verified or vouched for, and there is usually no knowing whether these are "phantom" or genuinely incurred. This problem is periodically raised, but again in 1999 the EP voted not to tighten up the system by requiring proper accounting verification procedures. So the lax, wasteful and fraudulent system is allowed to continue without remonstration from the other EU institutions.

The Council

The Council continues in the same pattern as before, with the Heads of Government, or the relevant Ministers according to subject matter, meeting regularly, and with most of its decisions virtually decided beforehand by the Officials of the Committee of Permanent Representatives (COREPER).

Amsterdam introduced (Article 7) a new power for the Council to **suspend** "certain of the rights", including the **voting** rights, of a State, if that State is in "serious and persistent breach" of principles mentioned in the new Article 6 (1). The latter Article is of the all-embracing, imprecise "motherhood and apple pie" variety: "The Union is founded on the principles of liberty, democracy, respect for human rights and fundamental freedoms, and the rule of law, principles common to the Member States". A proposal under Article

7 can be made by one-third of the Member States or the Commission (some measure of the Commission's power?) and after obtaining the EP's consent. The identity of "certain of the rights" which may be suspended is completely undefined and the principles of Article 6 (1) are so wide-open to a range of interpretation, that this further increment of power to the three main EU institutions — Council, Commission and Parliament — holds an element of potential menace.

The Treaty introduces provisions on **Common Foreign and Security Policy** in which the Council and the Commission will have a big role to play. The Council may, and surely will, request the Commission to submit proposals, and the Council is to recommend common strategies to the European Council, and shall adopt common positions and implement them. The Member States shall ensure that their national policies **conform** to the common positions, thus subordinating Member States to the EU in these vital areas. In this work, the Council Presidency will be assisted by the Secretary General of the Council who will function as High Representative for the common foreign and security policy.

This policy heading (see particularly Articles 13 to 18) is to include the progressive framing of a **common defence policy**, which may lead to a **common defence**. It also promotes closer relations with the **Western European Union** (WEU), with a view to integrating it into the EU. This provision fosters the progressive development of the WEU, and the diminishment of NATO.

The traditional secretiveness of the institutions is being somewhat relaxed. Article 255 provides that any EU citizen shall have the right of access to documents of the EP, the Council and the Commission, subject to grounds of public or private interest, which limits shall be determined by the Council. Under Article 207, the Council shall define the cases when it is acting in its legislative capacity and in those cases it is willing to allow greater access of the public to documents concerning the results of votes, explanations of votes and statements in the minutes. Similarly, in the interest of transparency and better organization, under Protocol No. 9 on the role of national Parliaments, the Commission is bound to forward promptly to national Parliaments and Governments all Commission consultation documents and Commission proposals for legislation.

The Court of Justice and the Court of Auditors

The **Court of Justice** continues its original role of watchdog, guardian, interpreter and enforcer of the Treaties. Contrary to English concepts of equity and natural justice, the Court gives its judgments with retrospective effect, which in some cases imposes vast financial obligations on Member States' governments, which emphasizes the latter's subordination and loss of sovereignty. The Court's procedure also requires all judgments to be unanimous (notionally anyway), and dissenting views are not published. The Court's jurisdiction has been amplified to allow it to give preliminary rulings on the validity and interpretations of framework decisions and to review the legality of actions by the EU and Member States on the grounds of lack of competence, the misuse of powers, or failure to fulfil a Treaty obligation, and has power to impose **fines** on States for such breaches.

The **Court of Auditors'** right of access to information needed for its audit of the EU accounts of all revenue and expenditure, including the European Investment Bank's activity in this regard, has been slightly improved under Article 248. However, if the Court finds irregularities (usually misappropriation and fraud) and reports on them, as it is under a duty to do, it still has no power to take remedial steps, and there is still no mechanism for this Court to be able to put in motion any corrective or punitive action.

Chapter Six

ENLARGEMENT

I do not believe that the progress of European integration should be based on expectations that 'European' feelings will be stronger than national identities
Vaclav Klaus, former Prime Minister of the Czech Republic, 1997

From the perspective of those pressing for access, the EU's approach has been marked by persistent reluctance amounting almost to denial that enlargement was a priority, a minimalist attitude to financial assistance, vulnerability to protectionist lobbies on market access, and above all a refusal to offer any timetable for membership
William Wallace, *Opening the Door*

To assist the development of agriculture in the Central and Eastern European Countries, the EU should relax the restrictions on imports to the EU from the CEECs
Report in June 1996 of the House of Lords Select Committee on the European Communities

In terms of the overall contribution, from a budgetary perspective our priority is to ensure that the 1.27 percent 'Own Resources' [EU Budget] ceiling covers the full cost of enlargement to all the ten applicants plus Cyprus
Helen Liddell, Economic Secretary to the Treasury, in evidence to the House of Lords Select Committee on the European Communities, 1997

The EU is a developing unitary State with a serious "democratic deficit" currently undergoing the colossal gamble of the single currency. Another gamble of similar, probably greater, proportions but different nature is **enlargement** of the EU by its being joined by ten ex-Communist countries in Central and Eastern Europe which may take place over the next decade or two, and maybe sooner. Reference to enlargement in the Treaty is limited and neutral. Article 49 is merely permissive, allowing any European State respecting the principles of liberty, democracy, human rights and the rule of law to apply for membership. The Preamble in neither of the Consolidated Treaties of Maastricht or Rome (you will recall from the earlier chapter on the Treaties that the provisions of Amsterdam are grafted into the two Consolidations) has anything precise or explicit regarding enlargement, but some vague general phrases may be interpreted as being capable of bearing that intention. The EU seems ambivalent on the subject. Member States feel that for geopolitical reasons they should enlarge, but at the same time they all realize that the process will create enormous difficulties and costs, and a number of States, especially those in receipt of large support under CAP and the Structural and Cohesion Funds, feel greatly threatened. The EU with its dirigiste centralized forms of control and trade protectionism is not interested in creating a free trade area, but is determined to impose its existing system on any new entrants. How this will go down with the various ex-Communist countries who have applied for EU Membership whilst trying to establish their own democratic institutions and free trade economies is uncertain. One suspects that the more they read the small print of the joining terms and the acquis communautaire, and the implications sink in, they are likely to become more and more sceptical and disenchanted.

There are ten Central and Eastern European Countries (CEECs) seeking to join, and the EU have sorted these into two groups. The first comprises the Czech Republic, Poland, Hungary, Slovenia and Estonia, plus Cyprus; and the second is: Slovakia, Bulgaria, Romania, Latvia and Lithuania. Leaving aside Cyprus, all ten CEECs have a low GDP and per capita income. The combined GDP of the ten CEECs is **less than 4%** of that of the EU States, and according to the House of Lords Select Committee Report of 1997 it will take 25 years for the average GNP of the applicant CEECs to reach **half** the average GNP of EU States. However, several of the CEECs have competitive economies in terms of low labour costs. In contrast, the EU has much higher GDP levels, but also has high labour costs and poor economic growth and is trailing in world markets. The EU already has serious budgetary difficulties, and the entry of new Member States would greatly exacerbate this problem. The CEEC applicants would all apply for substantial aid from CAP and structural funds, which would place huge strains on the EU Budget. It is therefore not surprising that France, Belgium and Italy, some of the States which would suffer reduced grants and subventions as a result of enlargement, attached a Declaration to the Amsterdam Treaty emphasizing the need for institutional reform **before** enlargement — "reinforcing the institutions", as the Declaration describes it.

The UK wish to preserve the present EU Budget ceiling of 1.27% of EU GNP, and this accords with the proposal of the Commission and the wishes of most EU Agricultural Ministers. The Commission has estimated the 1999 total EU GNP at £4954 billion, so at **1.27%, the EU Budget ceiling** is roughly £63 billion, (of which the UK contributes a gross share of some £9 billion). It is reported that some 80% of the EU Budget is earmarked for CAP subsidies and various agricultural and other subventions. It would appear that if the CEEC applicants are to receive any CAP and other fund payments, either the current recipients amongst the present Member States will have to suffer substantial reductions in payments, or the EU Budget will have to surge far above the present ceiling. Thus, in advance of the final decisions on enlargement, the EU will face a fundamental problem of crisis proportions. It is clearly vital that this dilemma be faced and resolved **before** any enlargement is undertaken. To give some perspective to the EU Budget ceiling figure, the Commission's own MacDougall Report of 1977, which mainly examined three unitary States (the UK, France and Italy) and five federal States (the USA, Canada, West Germany, Switzerland and Australia), found that central Government budgets in unitary States consumed an average of 45% of GDP, and in federal States a figure of between 20-25% of GDP. The Report concluded that the EU Budget was far too small and should be raised to a figure **at least between 5 - 7% of total GDP**, with a **further 4%** if common defence became a federal responsibility. It follows that during the federal integration process over the coming years, further increases in the EU Budget will have to be made, perhaps arriving at a figure of between 10-20% of total GDP — say, **more than ten times greater** than the present contributions of Member States.

There has been ample time — decades anyway, and some would say centuries — to realize the wholly disparate nature of all the fifteen Member States from each other. The proposed next ten Members will add a giant extra dimension of difference. Ten relatively poor countries with a total population of over 100 million, having recently thrown off the shackles of Communist rule over decades and striving to reorient themselves along democratic and free market lines are seeking to subsume themselves in a dirigiste oligarchy where democratic accountability is claimed but absent. I hope, for their sakes, as well as for the existing Members, that the whole enterprise will not turn into a case of 'out of the frying pan into the fire'. Vaclav Klaus, former Czech Republic Prime Minister, saw parallels between systemic shortcomings in the EU and in the ex-Communist States of Eastern Europe, which he expressed at a World Economic Forum in 1997: "The key question is how successful will be the dismantling of over-regulated and over-paternalistic welfare States in Western Europe. I do not know whether we will succeed in winning the battle with over-legislation and with corporatism and syndicalism in ourselves. I am afraid that both tendencies are deeply rooted in the intrinsic fabric of our societies. To extrapolate in 1997, the year 2007 is not a very rosy picture".

But the EU Budget is not the only problem area. The EU will foist onto the CEEC applicants the full burden of the acquis communautaire. This is the huge and evergrowing volume of acquired EU "competence" and powers which are wielded against Member States by the EU institutions. Since the UK became a Member in 1973 the number of regulations, directives and legal acts has increased from under 2000 to over 23,000 and the acquis extends to some 300,000 pages. To administer this outpouring of legislation, the Commission's staff has increased by tenfold. Likewise, the UK's civil service, as with the other Member States, has proliferated and spends a major part of its time administering Brussels legislation. The ten CEEC applicants, it is estimated, will have to increase their civil services by between ten-and twenty-fold, especially in their Agriculture Ministries, to cope with administering the Brussels acquis. Thus, if the envisaged enlargement takes place, the 15 present and the 10 new Members will have hundreds of thousands, perhaps millions, of civil servants spending their time on the non-productive, wasteful occupation of operating the diktats of the Brussels central government.

The Common Agriculture Policy will certainly be a massive stumbling block, as most of the EU Agricultural Ministers are unwilling to permit any reform. Several of the CEECs have prominent agricultural industries but find trading with EU Members very difficult because of Brussels protectionism and tariffs which make CEEC produce uncompetitive. Because of these measures, the EU is exporting more in the agricultural sector to the CEECs than the latter can export to the EU. German agricultural produce has a 50% subsidy whereas Polish produce has a mere 15% subsidy. In October 1997 in evidence to the House of Lords Select Committee, the German Foreign Minister said the German attitude would be that they "are for enlargement, but no Polish potatoes, not one", and a similar message would be repeated on other products by various Member States. The EU has already been irritating the CEECs and Russia by dumping on them heavily subsidized agricultural produce and by imposing anti-dumping duties on imports from those countries.

Because of the early stage in the development of their economies, the CEECs are unlikely to qualify as Members of EMU for many years after joining the EU. Will the new ERM (set up in June 1997 by the European Council) apply to them? Will they be obliged to submit to fiscal and economic disciplines unsuitable for their economies? The portents are that Brussels will compel all new applicants to take on the whole paraphernalia of its rules and obligations as a condition of Membership.

Another issue which should be of the greatest concern to CEECs is the pervasive incubus of **unfunded pensions** amongst the EU. This Damoclean risk hangs over all present and any future Members of the EU. Brussels claims that a Member State shall not be liable for the commitments of another Member, as stated in Article 103. Whilst such a liability would not fall **directly** on the other Members, at least under the present Treaties, a massive shortfall in funding by one State would cause that State to undergo large-scale borrowing, with a knock-on effect in interest rates for all Members, and perhaps other adverse repercussions. The calculation of government deficits and debt for the Maastricht Convergence Criteria (MCC) does not include any provision for state pension liabilities, so that if the latter became actual rather than prospective, the liable State would be in breach of the MCC and infringing the Stability Pact, thus becoming subject to its heavy financial penalties. A number of States are in the danger zone of unfunded pensions for the years ahead, and the already lax discipline of the MCC and Stability Pact might be eroded, leading to the unravelling and collapse of the whole structure of the single currency and EMU.

Another difficulty is the question of **languages**. Under the present Treaties, 12 languages are officially recognized, with all the complications and expense of interpretation, translation, printing and publishing. The CEEC applicants, if accepted, would introduce another ten languages. There are already some 2000 translators and

500 interpreters, and these numbers would have to be more or less doubled. It will become progressively more and more difficult to find enough interpreters and translators of sufficiently high calibre to do the job efficiently. It is always extremely difficult, and sometimes impossible, to communicate nuances and shades and subtle differences of meaning across language frontiers, and many misunderstandings can and do arise through imperfections in this field, sometimes through downright poor interpretation. This will be a growing risk. A huge expansion of bureaucracy would take place in all the EU institutions, as well as in new Member States, and to some extent in the present Members as well. The major States in the present Membership each promote their own language as hard as they can, and the French are furious about the way English is becoming established as the main language of the EU. With potentially ten more Members, for reasons of streamlining, economy and practicability, it may become desirable if not essential for the EU to limit the number of languages which may be used for official EU business. This would be likely to cause considerable friction amongst Members, particularly those who felt disadvantaged.

Other aspiring candidates are or were Malta, Cyprus and Turkey. The case of **Malta** was apparently straightforward, until its previous Government had a change of heart in October 1996 and withdrew its application, only to have its application reactivated on a change of Government in September 1998. It is strange for **Cyprus** to have been seen as being in the first wave of applicants. It is reported that the 1960 Treaty of Guarantee signed by the UK, Greece, Turkey and Cyprus will not permit Cyprus to join the EU. Bearing in mind the tensions between Greece and Turkey, it is hard to see the Treaty stumbling block being overcome, at least in the foreseeable future. In any event, Cyprus being divided in two parts, Greek and Turkish, since the Turkish invasion in 1974, would surely present problems. The case of **Turkey** as a candidate is a complicated one. That country has been on the waiting list longer than any other, and it is an important member of NATO, with the attendant western orientation. On the other hand, Turkey is a Muslim country, and is accused of human rights violations against the Kurdish people who inhabit lands part of which are Turkish. Also, Turkey and Greece are historically at odds with each other. Turkey is sensitive about its long wait, and its Prime Minister said after the December 1997 Luxembourg Summit that it might withdraw its membership application. Again, in June 1999 at the Cologne Summit Turkey's bid for candidature was rejected. However, Finland which began its six-month EU Presidency at the beginning of July 1999, said it wished to add Turkey to the new wave of applicants, although it may be expected that Greece would block such a move.

There are those who may believe that Turkey as a strategic and useful member of NATO weighs more in the balance of post-war European history than Greece as a member of EU. There is no doubt that **NATO** is a vital organization for the stability and protection of the western world. NATO is not co-extensive with the EU. NATO membership embraces all the EU except four neutral States: Ireland, Sweden, Finland and Austria; its core Atlantic countries are the USA, Canada and Iceland, and it extends to Turkey, Norway and the three new members Poland, the Czech Republic and Hungary which joined in March 1999. France is a member, although de Gaulle removed it from the integrated military command in 1966. In 1997 a Joint Permanent Council was founded between NATO and Russia, whereby Russia has a voice but not a veto in Alliance decision-making. Yet Russian wariness may make it difficult for Slovenia, Slovakia, Romania and Bulgaria to join NATO for several years. The chances of NATO membership for Lithuania, Latvia and Estonia — the countries in most need of NATO's protection — seem distant, because of Russia's suspicions.

The Western European Union too is now a hybrid creature. It started life as the Brussels Treaty Organization (BTO) under the Brussels Treaty of 1948 between the UK, France and the Benelux countries, for collective self-defence. With the collapse of the European Defence Community and the decision of NATO to incorporate West Germany into the Western security system, the BTO became the WEU in October 1954 with the admission of West Germany and Italy. Owing to its overlap with NATO, WEU went into suspended animation, until it was revitalized in the Maastricht Treaty. Under Maastricht (Article 17 and Declaration No. 3 and Protocol No. 1), increased importance is accorded to WEU and its likely future integration into the EU. The objective is that WEU will become the EU's defence component, with a commitment to harmonize views on defence and security and to create a European Security and Defence Identity. Various grades of association developed over the years up to 1996 when WEU had 10 EU full members, with the remaining five (Austria, Denmark, Finland, Ireland and Sweden) as observers, 3 Associate Members (Norway, Turkey, Iceland), and 10 Associate Partners (Bulgaria, Czech Republic, Estonia, Hungary, Latvia, Lithuania, Poland, Romania, Slovakia, Slovenia). A Council of Ministers with foreign and defence responsibilities meets twice a year in the presiding State, and Permanent Representatives under the WEU Secretary-General meet weekly. The Assembly of the WEU comprising 115 MEPs of Member States meets twice a year in Paris. At a NATO Summit in Berlin in June 1996, NATO agreed to allow a "European pillar" to be set up within the NATO Alliance, whereby operations could be conducted in NATO's name and using its structures and assets, but without the participation of the USA. Insofar as this decision might allow such operations to be conducted under the political and strategic direction of WEU, it was seen by some, including the French, as a diminution of the USA's influence and participation in NATO. France then promptly announced its readiness to resume its full part in NATO, after 30 years of limited membership. This decision also pleased Russia, for whom any steps taken by WEU and the EU to loosen the ties with the USA are gratifying. However, at the 50th anniversary of NATO held in April this year, in Washington, its official communiqué signed by the 19 NATO government leaders showed no signs of reducing USA influence. In future it is possible for a military operation to be carried out by the EU using NATO troops, structures and military assets under the command of the Deputy Supreme Commander, Europe, who is always a European and at present is British. One view is that this would pre-empt EU moves to build up a separate Euro-army, which would help to distance the USA from NATO. Assurances have been given that under the new arrangements defence will remain strictly a matter of **intergovernmental** cooperation and decision, with no role for the EU institutions or WEU; but past experience makes one wonder how long it will be before those institutions manoeuvre themselves into the forefront. In spite of the antipathy towards the USA on the part of some EU Members, particularly France, it seems strategically unwise and inept of such Members to make moves towards distancing the USA from NATO. **In a world of many unstable situations and volatile countries and organizations, to depreciate the alliance with the only superpower is ill-judged and unstatesmanlike**.

The problems and tensions of the existing EU are almost certain to be heightened by the addition of new Members. A Report on Enlargement published by the Centre of Finnish Business and Policy Studies in 1997 observed that bringing in the CEECs would involve particular political, economic and cultural stresses emphasized by their recent historical experience. The CEECs may look at **individual** EU Members and recognize them as desirably democratic, but on early acquaintance may not realize that the **amalgam of the EU itself** is a dirigiste centralized control system with an almost total democratic deficit. This they will surely come to recognise ever more clearly, the more their Governments and officials study the Treaties and the ever-increasing Acquis to which they must submit. The greater the disparity of the Membership, the wider the powers of the centralized Government (the Commission) will have to be, in order to preserve and advance the EU Socialist model. There will have to be accretions to all the EU institutions — the numbers of representatives in the Council, the Parliament, the Commission, the Court of Justice, the Court of Auditors and various other bodies will all grow, together with some reductions in the numbers of the MEPs of existing Members. In the Commission, new Directorates will no doubt be needed, new posts created, many reallocated. There will surely be a call, if not a need, for more staff in all Directorates and Secretariats. All this turmoil and change will cause great friction and ill-feeling amongst all Members existing and new — and immense extra cost.

If the CEECs are accepted by and sign up with the EU, they will do so believing it will be better to be part of a soi-disant democratic Union of the West than either remain an Eastern European enclave or fall again under the communist influence of the ex-Soviet States, but such a belief might prove to be ill-founded. It will be very sad for them if they find that they have committed themselves to being second-rate and burdened Members for many years to come in a tightly controlled, corrupt central bureaucracy with high unemployment, an economy falling behind in world markets, and a protectionist trade regime.

Chapter Seven

UK INTERNAL ISSUES
INTERACTING WITH THE EU

Devolution, and the Regions

Scotland has created an elected Parliament and Government with various though not total law-making powers and substantial continuing monetary subventions from the Government in Westminster. Whether the Scottish Nationalist Party persuade the Scottish people they really want independence from the UK Union created in 1707 remains to be seen. Wales too has achieved an elected Assembly, though not comparable in scope with the Scottish Parliament. Whether this Assembly succeeds in upgrading itself to Parliamentary status in the years ahead also remains to be seen. If Scotland eventually reaches the stage of independence, it will then clearly seek acceptance as an independent member of the EU. Even with their present respective statuses, Scotland and Wales fall tidily into the **regionalisation plans** of the Brussels blueprint. England itself is divided into eight Euro-regions. Earlier I referred to a private meeting in Chichester in September 1995. Other similar meetings will have taken place since then, including one reported at Brighton in April 1998. Representatives of local authorities and business gathered to discuss the "Future of Europe and Your Area", with lectures from the Brussels Committee of the Regions on "The South-East as a coherent Region of Europe". This is no doubt happening in all eight regions of England, and in Scotland and Wales too, to highlight "regional identity" and encourage direct links with Brussels to by-pass central government. Each region now has an office in Brussels. One can get in touch with the European Commission Representation in London and ask for the relevant regional booklet South East or otherwise, each one being described as a region of the European Union. Professor Manfred Dammeyer is President of the **Committee of the Regions** (Articles 263-265) which was set up under the Maastricht Treaty and holds five plenary sessions a year in the Parliament building in Brussels. In addition to the President and his office and secretariat, there are two or three Vice-Presidents from each of the 15 Member States, five Directorates and eight mini-Commissions, each with their staffs. Towards the end of 1998 Professor Dammeyer said that the setting up of regional "assemblies" for Scotland, Wales and Northern Ireland was a first step, with one to follow for London. The eight English Euro-regions have already been provided with inchoate core governments by means of **Regional Development Agencies** and there is now a Government Minister for Regions. The plan is to divide the larger nation states into smaller units with a strong sense of Community identity, and each regional government will have a regional chamber, in order to assist the concepts of the nation state and national identities to diminish. During the passage through Parliament of the Regional Development Agencies Bill, MPs seem to have been gripped by a general amnesiac paralysis as to how this development related to Brussels' "Europe of the Regions" scheme.

On the **twinning of towns** in EU States, one might indulgently view them as an excuse for an exchange of light-hearted visits between local councillors, but one can get a booklet from the Commission or its UK office entitled *A Europe of Towns and Cities, A Practical Guide to Town-twinning*. This will show that twinning is yet another weapon in the Commission's extensive armoury for the promotion of European integration. At the twinning ceremony, the mayors are to take the "oath", a promise to "join forces to help secure, to the utmost of our abilities, a successful outcome to this vital venture of peace and prosperity — European Union". If the precise wording of the preferred version is not used, "whatever version is used must make clear that European unification is the primary aim of and reason for the twinning". Every action of the Commission, however innocent-looking, has the ulterior motive of eventual federal union.

Race Relations

Maastricht has been expanded in the Amsterdam Treaty (Articles 29 - 42) to provide for the protection of the citizen "by developing common action... in the fields of police and judicial cooperation in criminal matters and by preventing and combating **racism and xenophobia**..." "through closer cooperation between police forces, customs authorities and other competent authorities, both directly and through the European Police Office (Europol)". Also, under Article 13 the EU Council, acting unanimously, can adopt measures to act against discrimination based on racial or ethnic origin, as well as on sex, religion, disability, age or sexual orientation. Every EU Member has immigration and race problems of different sorts and degrees, and how far a centralized source of regulation and control will be helpful or counterproductive remains to be seen. In the UK the Race Relations Act, the Race Relations Board, the Commission for Racial Equality, and proliferating bodies for equal opportunities and civil rights and liberties of all kinds are building up a situation which at some stage may be ripe for a backlash from the 95% of the total UK population who are not ethnic or other minorities. At the heart of the April 1999 Macpherson Report is the extreme view that "A racist incident is any incident which is perceived to be racist by the victim or any other person". This widely criticized Report has a lasting tendency to encourage ethnic minority sensitivies to even higher levels, and so any ensuing activities are likely to impact more on the ambit of the Treaty provisions and of the European Court of Human Rights. No-one should wish, nor the Government allow, the exploitation of racism by pressure groups.

Northern Ireland

The same section of the Amsterdam Treaty, particularly Article 29, also seeks to provide citizens with a high level of safety by developing common action in preventing and combating **terrorism**

and illicit arms trafficking (amongst other things). Viewed in the EU perspective, it is surely bizarre that one EU Member State should be host country to several hundred terrorists — their own nationals — who, with insufficient restraint from their hosts, have over many years bombed, shot, murdered, kidnapped and maimed the citizens of a sister EU Member State. These terrorists declare that they are "at war" with the other Member State, though their host State is at peace with that State, and the terrorists have in their armouries in many sites around their host country large quantities of mortars, artillery, ground-to-air missiles, Semtex explosive and a range of automatic weapons and small arms, more than enough to justify the word "war", certainly guerrilla war.

Since Partition in 1992, the six Northern counties of Ulster have remained part of the UK with a clear Protestant majority. The future of Ulster depends on the wishes of the majority, as in any democracy, and that principle must be treated as sacrosanct by any British Government, and also by the Irish.

As a token of its power as a burgeoning central government, the EU Commission could flex its muscles under Article 29 and other Treaty terms and press the Irish Government to take much stronger action against the IRA, using the array of information about the IRA which is common to all the parties and their services. In addition to the terrorism and illicit arms trafficking provisions of Article 29 (Consolidated Maastricht), there are Articles 6 and 7 of the same Treaty. These provisions authorize the Council to suspend rights, including voting rights, of a Member State which is in "serious and persistent breach" of the principles of liberty, democracy, respect for human rights and fundamental freedoms and the rule of law. There are also sanctions in Articles 226-228 (Consolidated Rome) whereby the Commission or a Member State may take a Member State to the Court of Justice if that State has failed to fulfil an obligation under the Treaty, and if the Court finds accordingly, it may impose a "lump sum or penalty payment" on that State. Apart from these processes, as humanitarian and peaceful co-existence considerations are clearly not enough, Ireland as one of the biggest beneficiaries of CAP subsidies and Structural and Cohesion fund handouts, would not like its very considerable benefits threatened or withdrawn, nor to be the focus of EU pressure and critical attention.

Chapter Eight

ATTITUDES: GOVERNMENT AND THE PEOPLE

Europe really doesn't matter that much
Michael Heseltine, former Deputy Prime Minister,
on the BBC *Today* programme, 28 June 1999

There is no act of treachery or meanness of which a political Party
is not capable. For in politics there is no honour
Benjamin Disraeli

...the British people should know where they are going before they
wake up and find themselves where they do not want to be
Anthony Eden, former Foreign Secretary and Prime Minister

The great masses of the people ... will more easily fall victims
to a great lie than to a small one
Adolf Hitler, *Mein Kampf*

The creation of a single European State bound by one European
Constitution is the decisive task of our time
Joschka Fischer, German Foreign Minister, November 1998

Nevertheless, in contrast: Europeans will never become a homogeneous
nation State because of differences in peculiarities, languages, history,
prejudices, passions and animosities
Joschka Fischer, November 1998

Peace, commerce and honest friendship with all
nations — entangling alliances with none
Thomas Jefferson, inaugural address, March 1801

I have earlier commented on the chameleon-like changing attitudes over the years since World War II of Governments and individual leaders and Ministers, and it has also been and still is the case that significant proportions of the Party in power at any particular time have held views on the Community different from their own Government. Although there has always been an astonishing degree of ignorance about the Community in Government and Parliamentary circles, open dissent has largely been muted, owing to the Parliamentary Whip. However, it seems to be the case at present that in the Labour Party there are many who are anti-single currency and anti-EU, and in the Opposition there are a number who are pro-single currency and pro-EU. At present, too, Prime Minister Tony Blair seems wholeheartedly to embrace his prospect of joining the single currency and EMU with all its implications, as well as the continuing advance towards integration and federal union. One cannot tell if or when this enthusiasm will wane or wither, but now it seems firm and set. In passing, one may wonder whether and to what extent Government and Party leaders design and engineer policy for the good of the country, or the Party, or their own career, or in what permutation of these objectives. It is said that Blair fancies himself as President of the Commission later on, which post in the years ahead will turn into the President of the European Union alias the United States of Europe.

It is a constant mystery how far or how little our leaders and their teams read or are aware of the Treaties and the cataclysmic changes they make in our lives and the whole fabric of our society. I was hesitantly prepared to believe that in the late 1940s and 1950s the true political intentions of the original Six were kept from our leaders, although in view of Lord Thorneycroft's unattractive argument in his pamphlet *Design for Europe* that is perhaps naive of me. He wrote of the overcoming of obstacles to European Union, and opined that the plan to be adopted, even on the purely economic level, was too vast to be prepared in detail before being undertaken, and would have to be modified "as we go". If this pamphlet was considered by the Labour Cabinet of the time (1947) or by the following Conservative Governments, then this dishonest policy of concealing the **sacrifices** inherent in any plan and leading the people "slowly and unconsciously" into the abandonment of their traditional liberties and independence, has been the central plank of Government European policy ever since. One is amazed at the facility politicians have for denying or shutting out obvious facts, but this habit (disease?) is endemic amongst the breed. Avoidance of factual reality goes hand in hand with secrecy, to quarantine truth from the people. This disagreeable Orwellian practice shows that **Governments have always known that the people deeply but undemonstratively wish not to surrender their historic island birthright as an independent nation.**

This long-standing willingness by the Government of the day to go along, with reluctance or empressement, with the Community gamble, stems from a lack of confidence and faith in their own country. This in turn has largely been continued by the **invertebrate policy of the Foreign Office** over decades since at least the 1960s when Burke Trend's Cabinet paper (previously referred to) expressed timid concern for the UK's future if outside the Community. This attitude congealed into party lines based on false and unworthy mantras such as "there is no alternative", this is "inevitable", if we don't do this we'll "miss the train", we "must not get left behind", and so on. This approach is **defeatist, abject and false**. Other fanciful and unrealistic concepts include "being at the very heart of Europe", and "the ability to influence the future course of the EU into more free-market ways", and "we will suffer much loss of influence if we are outside". The same threadbare myths are trundled out by defeatist past Ministers like Howe, Heseltine and Clarke, as well as by the inexperienced Labour "new boys". The flaccid credulity in their adopting these false notions and the limp submissiveness in their feeling bound to go along with the EU ever-deepening integration and federalism is contemptible and should be scorned by all.

During the 1990s there has developed on the continent an ever-greater openness, now rising to a crescendo, about the federal goal, to a point over the last year or two where even the most purblind can not fail to be aware of it. Up to a few years ago the British public's attitude, if such it can be called, was one of semi-conscious unformed fatalism that this whole Community process was "inevitable". But, though late in the day, this recent clamour has caused a flicker and more recently a growing pulse in the public consciousness, and signs of a gradual shift out of the national stasis are discernible. Indeed, recent polls have shown that a majority of the population do not want to join the single currency, and that a substantial, and growing, minority wish the UK to leave the EU altogether. It is to be hoped that the people generally can be persuaded, and as soon as possible, to grasp the significance of the enormous issues at stake. In the last few years, numerous groups covering top businessmen, MPs, peers, trades union leaders, academics, economists, members of the professions, journalists, consumer associations and others have been gaining a higher profile. **The European Research Group** (ERG) have been holding in Westminser a series of half-yearly Congresses for Democracy at which over thirty anti-euro Groups attend mainly representing MPs, Trades Unions and business. There is also the anti-euro group New Europe, chaired by Lord Owen, which in the autumn of 2000 announced that they were joining forces with Business for Sterling. Both these anti-euro Groups have a large following of hundreds of business leaders and major companies. Then there is the rival, pro-euro group Britain in Europe, supported by the Government, Heseltine and Clarke, and many businesses. This group has not been so prominent since the continuing dire performance of the euro and the Conservative successes in the European elections in June 1999. A propos of those elections, the BBC's ill-concealed Labour sympathies, at odds with its Charter obligations of impartiality, were again evidenced in that context. The company Minotaur Media Tracking for hundreds of hours for five weeks up to election day 10th June 1999 monitored the news bulletins of BBC 1, BBC 2, Radio 4, and ITV. Minotaur's Report showed that markedly disproportionate time, emphasis and significance were given in favour of the pro-euro interests. The British public have the right to expect and require from the media, and particularly from the BBC as public service broadcasters, impartiality and fair play in reportage and presentation, especially on matters of vital national importance.

Although there are nuances and variations on all sides, there seem mainly to be four broad strands in the approach to the single currency and EMU. These four preferred positions, in over-simplified and abbreviated form, are:

(i) in the single currency/EMU; in the EU, and federal;

(ii) in the single currency/EMU; in the EU, but not federal;

(iii) outside the single currency/EMU; in the EU, but not federal;

(iv) outside the single currency/EMU; outside the EU.

Tony Blair and Labour are calamitously in the **first** category, with seeming enthusiasm; William Hague and the Conservative Party are in the **third** category. Lord Beloff the eminent historian in his book *Britain and European Union Dialogue of the Deaf* sums up in a sentence in simplified terms the position in stance (i) above, and then that in stance (iv), as follows:- "Either one has to accept the ultimate defeatism of Edward Heath and his friends, and say that in the contemporary world an independent Britain makes no sense, and that if one's destiny is to be just one of the provinces of a federal system one should organise one's affairs so as to make the best of it; **or** one has to argue that Britain's material and human resources are such that if free to make her own policies through her own Parliamentary processes there is no need for such a sacrifice".

Chapter Nine

THE FUTURE?

*We are not prepared to accept the principle that the most vital
economic forces of this country should be handed over to an authority
that is utterly undemocratic and accountable to no-one*
Clement Attlee, Labour Prime Minister, 1950

*England is insular and maritime ... her nature, her structure, her
economic position differ profoundly from those of the continentals*
President de Gaulle of France, 1963

*How can you let a country with a great history for twenty generations
disappear as a province of a bureaucratic Euro State run by Helmut Kohl?
I don't understand what is wrong with you*
Pat Buchanan, American Presidential candidate
in 1996, and prospectively in 2000

*What matters to the people of this country, unless I have got them
wrong, is to be masters in their own house, to have the right to make
their own laws, settle their own taxes and change their own government.
That right will be taken away from them soon if they do not defend it*
Enoch Powell

*The British Parliament in Westminster retains the final right to repeal
the Act which took us into the Market on 1st January 1973. Thus our
continued membership will depend on the continuing assent of Parliament.*
Labour Government pamphlet *Britain's New Deal in Europe*
before the 1975 Referendum

England! awake! awake! awake!
William Blake

The defect of tunnel vision towards the EU

I am appalled by EU-novice Blair, in the appeasement tradition, having no confidence or belief in the UK as an independent nation, and thus failing us all as a national leader. Sadly Labour is not the only party which contains doubters and appeasers, and the Foreign Office seems riddled with them. Those who have no "faith and fire" for their country should not be in positions of authority. A heredity akin to appeasement runs from the 1930s intermittently through our political parties (not forgetting the Thorneycroft Paper) to Edward Heath who was the prime mover in starting the shameful rot, and numbers of leaders in both main Parties have since continued in the same timid capitulating state of mind. By what contorted thought process can they argue that this nation is in such a parlous condition that it must at all costs, and it would be **at all costs**, become a "mere province" (per Lord Beloff), just a "unit" (per Heath), a "rate-capped county council" (per Norman Ridley, former Minister) in the Federal Union of Europe? In fact, the opposite is the truth, but similarly to the Soviet method, this truth is denied, skirted, derided, abused, ignored. But in the EU context, the Government see everything **topsy turvy**. Because of their mental conditioning they fail to see that the UK would **gain** in influence and prestige and benefit outside the EU, rather than lose them. After all, the UK has been a Member State for 27 years and it cannot be said that it has gained influence over that time. And what about those 27 years? We joined, we were given to believe, for the benefits of the Common Market which turned into the Single Market, but Mario Monti, the Internal Market Commissioner in 1996, said: "The Single Market has not developed as we had hoped at the macro-economic level". The advantages of the Single Market have proved to be illusory, and the EU economy has shown itself to be uncompetitive, falling behind in world trade, owing to Brussels' protectionist "Fortress Europe" mentality and aversion to free trade. The UK has been one of the major net contributors to the EU budget, and has accumulated a massive trade deficit in the EU, whilst gaining a trade surplus in the world beyond the EU. The British people have been greatly penalised by the burden of artificially high food prices due to the outdated socialist policy of Brussels, particularly the CAP. A memorandum on CAP from the Ministry of Agriculture to the House of Lords Select Committee in 1995 gave the official view: "The huge cost of the policy to taxpayers and consumers far outweighs any benefit to them ... such large transfers into agriculture represent a major misallocation of resources and thus damage the economy as a whole ... the policy is extremely complex in detail, hence difficult and costly to administer and giving scope for fraud". The Common Fisheries Policy, rushed into existence just in time to catch Heath in his complaisant submission for entry to the Community, has been a ruinous disaster for our fishing industry and related workers. Our fishing fleet is decimated, many fishing families bankrupted, our historic fishing grounds removed from our jurisdiction, and the fishing stocks on the way to annihilation. Our highest Courts and our Acts of Parliament can be and have been overruled by the European Court of Justice. The VAT and other duties are governed by Brussels. Our working hours, wages and conditions are ordained by Brussels. We foolishly took a "great leap in the dark" in joining the Exchange Rate Mechanism (ERM), the precursor of the single currency which Malcolm Rifkind, former Foreign Secretary, described as "a catastrophe waiting to happen". Our two years in 1990-1992 in the ERM was indeed a catastrophe, during which period our unemployment rose, thousands of businesses went to the wall, thousands of homes were repossessed and the estimated cost of the whole deplorable episode was between £68 billion and £79 billion. The previous Government having dipped its toes in the water and having its foot severely burnt, this Government wants to do it all over again.

The Blair position

Blair gives the appearance of uncritically supporting everything communautaire and politically correct. He wishes the UK to join the single currency when he claims that, in his view, it is economically right for us. He persists in treating it as a purely economic problem, and refuses to answer any questions on the political and constitutional implications, in defiance of an Early Day Motion in Parliament pressing him to do so. He was heading for a referendum early after the next General Election, but after the weakness of the Euro and the considerable Conservative successes in the June 1999 Euro-elections he went to ground, but by August he was emerging from cover. If the Euro picks up to some extent, which may happen, and Germany improves in its own economic cycle, and if the Government spin, propaganda and disinformation machine can sufficiently hoodwink the people, on present indications Blair will probably go for an early referendum. If his stratagem works and he wins the referendum, he will take us all on **the most dangerous and fateful journey our country has yet taken**. It will not be a leap in the dark, because we have experienced it before in the ERM — the two ruinous years of 1990-92 — but not learnt from it. No excuses next time, just a conscious plunge into a high-cost, low-benefit state of dependency.

The single currency/EMU one-size-fits-all exchange rate and interest rate simply cannot suit all the 11 Members at the same time, let alone all the time, and the more Members there are, the worse it will function — 15, or 20, or 25, or even more in the future, if it lasts as long as that. Italy has already breached its Maastricht convergence criteria (MCC) limits, and has applied for, and received, permission to do so; this shows how "flexible" the Commission is willing to be and how disdainful of the provisions of the Treaty and of the Stability Pact criteria for punishing offenders. Several others of the 11 Members locked into the single currency are in breach or heading for breach of the criteria levels, and it remains to be seen how they are treated by the Commission. It is almost certain that all of the 11 Members will be straining and distorting their economies to "sustain" their criteria levels, as "sustainability" is required by the Treaty. If or when we join the single currency, we will have to hand over reserves of some £28 billion for the ECB to manage — not on our behalf — and the exchange rate and interest rate fixed for us may well be wrong for our economy. If by luck it is more or less correct for us at the beginning, it will surely become wrong for us later on in our own distinctive economic cycle, which is more akin to the USA than to Germany. In the straitjacket régime of the single currency/EMU, Members will from time to time, maybe at irregular intervals, **seesaw** up and down, with the Members on each side of the seesaw changing sides now and then as their separate differing economic cycles rotate. There will nearly always be some Members underperforming, and on the principle of "the speed of the convoy is the speed of the slowest ship", this will ensure that the EU as a whole will go on slipping behind in world trade.

This Government, and previous ones, have fostered the various **myths** about the UK's position, on the basis that the more they are repeated, the less they are analysed and seen through. This has maintained our collective sleep-walking further and further into the quicksand. "There is no alternative"; "we must not miss the train"; "if we don't join, we will lose influence and be left behind"; "if we are in, we can persuade them to make changes", and others. On this last vain hope, Lord Lamont, former Chancellor, said in 1995 in his book *Sovereign Britain*: "There is no argument in Europe. There is Britain's point of view, and there is the rest of Europe. There is not a shred of evidence at Maastricht or since that anyone accepts our view of Europe... The plain fact acknowledged by every continental politician — except those on the fringes of power — is that the other Members want a European State, whether they express it in these precise terms or not". On the "no alternative" myth, there **certainly is a multi-faceted alternative** which I will comment on later. But if there were no alternative, we would be left in a subordinate, uninfluential position as a mere province in an ever more centralized socialist bureaucracy, in which we would at some stage be shorn of our seat on the UN Security Council, on the World Bank, on the IMF, on the G7 group of industrial nations — all of which posts would probably pass to the President of the Commission as President of the Executive Government of the Federal Union. This would be sweet music to the French, and maybe to other Member States. On the "lose influence" myth, Sir Malcolm Rifkind, Foreign Secretary 1995-1997, wrote *(Sunday Telegraph,* 18th July 1999) that influence has to be measured in **global**, not just EU, terms. Influence is a means to an end, not an end in itself. It would be foolish to abandon our interests merely to retain our influence. Occasionally it may be right to accept a loss of influence if that is the only way to protect our interests. **The test must be of national interest**, not some vague yearning for influence. He suggested that if the UK decided to leave the EU, we would probably lose some influence in the EU, but overall we would gain more influence in global terms.

More powers are being given to the EU institutions, especially the Commission. However, Hans-Gert Poettering, leader of the biggest Parliament party the 232-member EPP, demanded that they see the second independent Report in the autumn of 1999, on Commission fraud, nepotism and mismanagement, before deciding whether or not to approve the appointment of Commission President Romano Prodi's new team. More national **vetoes** are going and will be traded away, compromised or circumvented. **Tax harmonization** is looming more persistently, with calls for business tax and VAT changes. The Code of Conduct working group of EU Finance Ministers chaired by the British Dawn Primarola is examining **200 measures of tax harmonization**, as they euphemistically put it, to eliminate "harmful tax competition". The all-party House of Lords Select Committee criticized the lack of "transparency" surrounding the work of this Working Group which showed up the Government in a very poor light. Their Report also said that this Code could lead to the UK being forced to accept tax measures damaging to the UK economy and its citizens. The

Government claim that the Code "is not legally binding", but this is merely a part of the standard three-stage Government method of warding off and stalling any public concern or opposition. **Stage one** is to deny the existence of the queried subject and to scoff at the enquiry and those raising it as fanciful and obsessive. **Stage two**, as in the case above, is to say that any threatened harmful legislation is only a talking point, a discussion paper, a position report, an exploratory draft, or a suggested guideline with no binding legal effect. **Stage three**, when after the usual EU and Government secrecy a regulation or decision sees the light of day, protests and queries are turned aside brusquely with the statement that the new rule is a fait accompli and it is too late to do anything. This is the standard dirigiste technique in Brussels and in the complaisant Governments of EU Members who practise the same stratagem. The feared **20% withholding tax** threat is merely stayed for the moment. According to the Wall Street Journal, in April 1998 the total foreign exchange market volume in London averaged around **£410 billion a day**, equal to the combined figure for New York, Tokyo and Singapore. The City of London won this vast business largely because the USA imposed a similar sort of withholding tax which drove the business away from New York. Now Brussels, which must be aware of this background, wish to impose this punitive impost, which would harm the EU as a whole, as well as do primary damage to London, by driving the forex trade either back to New York, or to some other non-EU centre such as Tokyo, Singapore or Zurich. Are the socialist centrist bigotry of Brussels and the anti-Anglo-Saxon animus so strong that harm to the EU is acceptable provided greater harm is done to the UK? Step by step, various forms of tax will be targeted. Other commodities and facilities will come within the frame for VAT harmonization. Business taxes, social insurance tax rates, and at some stage capital tax, and income tax — there have been calls recently for a EU income tax. The threat of introducing the **Corpus Juris**, a common EU juridical system, is awaiting a suitable time for being moved forward, and this will erode the English legal system which only the UK and Ireland share. The Euro-Parliament has voted in favour of the system of Corpus Juris which would do away with our historic rights of habeas corpus, trial by jury and the presumption of innocence. As mentioned earlier, there are plans for a European Public Prosecutor with its system of juridical criminal investigation to overlie our long-standing system. Also, the Government has signed up to a Directive on reversal of the burden of proof in sex discrimination whereby employers will be at added risk from claims by employees. More steps towards **Enlargement** are stalled for the time being, because further attempts to amend the CAP were unsuccessful through the intransigence of France and Germany. Finland, when holding the EU Presidency in 1999, tried to help Turkey in its application for Membership, and in July 1999, Joschka Fischer, the German Foreign Minister, said that Germany, who have two million resident Turks, are willing to assist as well. More scenes of tension and disagreement will take place about the **EU Budget**, and the UK will have to fight hard to defend its rebate, won by Mrs. Thatcher, from assault or demolition. Bearing in mind the Government's expressed desire to keep the EU Budget below the agreed ceiling of 1.27% of EU GDP, and the growing pressures for that limit to be exceeded, the whole Budget debate will be a continuing angry battleground. There are ongoing moves to inflate **the WEU** and integrate it into the EU, sidelining NATO. The mainly French-led EU antipathy towards the USA has been more evident since the collapse of the Soviet Empire in 1989, since when the EU has, wrongly, felt less need for strategic alliance with the one remaining world superpower, the USA. At the NATO Summit at Madrid in 1997, the European Security and Defence Identity (ESDI) was confirmed and the Combined Joint Task Force was established with the right to use NATO assets. In December 1998 at St. Malo the UK and France had an Accord on the Common Foreign Defence Policy (CFDP) leading to a **Common Defence Policy**, which in turn will, unless halted, develop into a single EU

Defence Force, and later on to a Euro army. Of course there will be many difficulties and differences about a **common foreign policy**, as many Member States have conflicting interests in many other countries, for example, Iraq, China, the African States, the Balkans, Poland, and the Middle East, to mention a few. These divergent considerations include oil, military equipment, agricultural produce and so on, as well as non-commercial matters such as culture, religion and human rights. For as long as the UK remains in the EU, whether or not we are in the single currency/EMU, the ominous shade of EU **unfunded pensions** hangs over all, involving untold cost and trouble. Recalling how our fishing waters and rights were surrendered by Heath without any negotiating resistance, we must hope that, by way of some deal or compromise, the Blair Government will not concede to Brussels our **oil and gas** interests as a "common European resource" in like fashion. The division of the EU into **Regions** is continuing. It is operated by the Committee of the Regions with a large Secretariat and its own Directorates, and liaison with Directorate General XVI, and hundreds of representatives from the Member States, of whom the UK has 24 representatives and 24 Alternates. This structure will progress and create closer ties between the Regional offices direct with Brussels, sidelining the national Governments.

Are all these costly dangers and drawbacks really being hazarded just for the will-o'-the-wisp "influence"? Blair wishes to "punch above his weight" in Brussels, which is understandable for a light-weight. But with his complaisance and eagerness in all things European, he seems prepared to commit this country all down the line. In any event, even if he felt like taking a more robust stance, he would not be allowed to alter the EU course. France and German are the EU axis and engine, a position reaffirmed in the Elysée Treaty of January 1963 between Chancellor Adenauer and President de Gaulle, and the EU's deeply ingrained federal intention is adamantine.

But, whilst one must try to believe otherwise, it almost seems as if Blair has an antipathy for the UK of historic traditions, values and composition. In all too many respects his performance seems to be acting out a wish-fulfilment of making the UK disunited, mediocre and indeterminate, so that it becomes more suitable as a mere dependency or group of regions in the multi-region bureaucratic Federal Union. He is gradually side-lining Parliament and adopting a more Presidential style of government, but without the control mechanisms of the USA by Congress and the Supreme Court. Blair and his Oval office are raising "spin" to an art form, substituting it and focus groups for true leadership. He is distancing Scotland, Wales and Northern Ireland, in different ways; he is dividing England (in more senses than one) into eight different Regions, each with its control structures, and all these Regions will be encouraged by the Commission to develop closer and closer links direct with Brussels, bypassing the national Government. He is failing to defend and support the police both here in England and the RUC in Ulster. He is failing to recognize and put an end to the harm being done in countryside issues by the ignorance and envy of city dwellers. He is failing to clamp down on the anarchic trouble-makers of the "rent-a-mob" tendency who cause great damage and mayhem whenever the opportunity arises, recently in the City and routinely at football matches. He is cutting back our T.A. reserve and regular armed forces and our Defence Budget to unacceptably low levels. He allows encouragement of positive discrimination in race and gender relations and concerning minority groups. He turns a blind eye to political partiality in the BBC (so long as it favours his Government) and to "dumbing down" across the media generally. He does not discourage the moves in education, particularly in the study of history and English literature, to ignore most of the important figures and events of the past and to concentrate on the 20th century in a sociological way. He allows the undermining of the family by often intrusive and authoritarian social services. He does not take firm steps to control or even moderate the chaotic state of immigration. All these failures are debasing our national way of life and are demeaning to the country, turning it into a **hotchpotch**. And it will be made even worse by "ever closer union" with the EU.

Part of Blair's armoury (though he is not unique in this) is what was revealingly described by a Cabinet Secretary as "economy with the truth". As just one example, regarding the Government's inept handling of the selling of the nation's gold reserves, in answer to a question in May 1999, Blair's answer, recorded in the Official Report, was that "throughout the world countries have been selling gold in order to diversify their reserves". Several days before that, the Governor of the Bank of France, Jean-Claude Trichet, said that the position of France, Germany, Italy and the USA, the four main holders of gold stocks in the world, is not to sell gold. It is also reported that of the more than 100 countries that hold gold, only five, with relatively small economies, have sold gold. These facts throw Blair's words into an entirely different light, and show his weasel words for what they are.

The advantages of being in the EU are few and slight. There is arguably some influence to be had in EU matters, but with the remaining vetoes and derogations sure to go with the passage of time and the addition of ten new Members, the voice of one of the "provinces" out of 15, 20 or 25 will not count for much; particularly so, as in that situation our global influence would probably diminish too. Our influence cannot be said to have grown during our 27 years of EU Membership. The Single Market has not been a great success. The proclaimed main benefit is in transaction costs, but these have been shown to be meagre and are far outweighed by the transition costs of preparing the country for the single currency which are running into many billions. We have a few optouts or derogations, won in bitterly hard-fought sessions. There was the Social Chapter optout obtained by the Conservative Government, but Blair's Government surrendered it, opening the floodgates to regulations for working hours, wage rates and related matters. There is our Schengen optout relating to cross-border control, won by the Conservatives. Owing to a mistake by Blair's officials, the UK cannot decide to "opt in" to the Schengen acquis without the unanimous agreement of the other Members. The main optout of real value to us is the one regarding the single currency/EMU, also won by the Conservative Government, but now awaiting surrender by Blair, subject to a referendum going his way and to his claiming that the economic conditions are adequate.

So looking at the position in the round, I suggest that the advantages of joining the single currency/EMU are negligible, whereas the disadvantages of so doing are many and enormous. In fact, the benefits of EU Membership itself are so shadowy as to prompt Lord Lamont, former Chancellor of the Exchequer, to say that: "when we came to examine the advantages of our Membership of the European Union they are remarkably elusive. As a former Chancellor I can only say I cannot pinpoint a single concrete economic advantage that unambiguously comes to this country because of our membership of the European Union". Indeed, it is apparent that 27 years in the Community have cost the UK very dear, and that the sensible Conservative aim of trying to retain some essential elements of independent nationhood have largely been unsuccessful against the hell-bent dirigiste machine of Brussels. Willing to sacrifice our people's historic heritage as an independent democratic nation for the parochial status of a province and an easier though less significant life in the EU, Blair has thrown in his lot with the EU Socialist adherents of the Brussels apparatchiks, all protectionist "Little Europeans" in their mind-set. Can we expect him to resist any of the many harmful measures being taken or threatened? Or have we only the prospect of oceans of hyperbole and bombast screening his ignominious kowtowing at every stage, step by step towards the Federal Union? His sickening efforts at self-promotion point to the latter as his future course of conduct.

The Hague position

Whilst I scorn Blair's accommodating attitude to Brussels and the

EU, I applaud Hague's desire to fight for his country in the EU forum and to stand up for the UK's independence. I believe Hague's instincts and inclinations about the single currency are sound, and that his Party's tactics will have to be ever more sure-footed. But I have deep concerns about the other part of his stance, which is being in the EU but not governed by it. In my view, this proposition is virtually a contradiction in terms. Hague does not swallow, as Blair is prepared to do, the baggage of socialist dirigisme, and so the UK would always remain the odd man out. The whole spirit and essence of the 50 year-old Socialist centrist bureaucratic model is immovably fixed and is not susceptible to change in favour of free-trade, independent ways. Hague's "à la carte Europe", as he outlined in May 1999 at Budapest, is just not available on the EU agenda. The Conservative Party Manifesto for the European Elections in June 1999, displayed a worthy and desirable wish-list including these points: Opposition to entry to the single currency. Opposition to further erosion of our veto. Opposition to harmonization of taxes. Support for NATO and opposition to a Euro-army. Opposition to a EU criminal justice system. Opposition to harmonization of road charges and transport tariffs. Opposition to a common immigration policy. Fight to reduce the EU Budget and the UK's net contribution to it. Fight to reduce bureaucracy and red tape. It is, I fear, true that there are negligible chances of success in most of the opposition and fighting outlined in this Manifesto. Before Hague continues for too long with the "in Europe, but not run by it" stance, he and his advisers should think further and very carefully about the changes needed to make staying in the EU a viable proposition, and weigh up the chances of the UK achieving all or any of them. If after thorough analysis Hague continues with his present policy, and the Conservative Party is returned to power at the next Election or the subsequent one, its then Government would have a constant struggle on its hands. Part of the struggle should be a task that Blair does not wish to take up, for fear of disturbing his cosy relationship with the French. The task is to check and cut back the predominance of the French in the Commission establishment and other key international organizations. Over the years French bureaucrats have been manoeuvred into many of the more important posts, and this was particularly achieved during Jacques Delors' tenure of the Commission Presidency in 1985-1995. Socialist Pascal Lamy, chief aide to Delors, is now chosen for the influential post of Commissioner of Trade. Nicole Fontaine, an arch-federalist, is the new President of the Euro-Parliament. And French officials have been allowed to treat as traditional fiefdoms the top post in the IMF, the OECD, and the European Bank of Reconstruction and Development (EBRD), and they have next call on the Presidency of the European Central Bank (ECB), after the current incumbent the Dutchman Wim Duisenberg. The French frequently get their way in the EU scene by behaving like temperamental prima donnas, and that is how they succeeded in having a totally unnecessary second Parliament building built at huge expense in Strasbourg, although the new building in Brussels is entirely suitable and continues to be the preferred venue to avoid the wasteful monthly pilgrimage of thousands of staff and MEPs from Brussels to Strasbourg.

Hague recognizes that **the ERM/single currency/EMU system is much more of a risk and danger to accept than to reject**, especially as its shortcomings are now more obvious, with Members breaching the convergence criteria with impunity. **Similarly, Hague, his Party and the country must come to realize that there is much greater risk and danger for the UK in staying in the EU than in leaving it.**

In the meantime, some of the Conservative party old-stagers, whose EU attitudes helped topple the last Government, are making their turncoat services available to Blair in a nauseating show of disloyalty. Patten chaired the Government-appointed group studying the RUC in Ulster, and as feared, this Report is adding to the stress and disadvantage which that harassed UK territory continues to undergo. Heseltine and Clarke are holding themselves ready to give public support to Blair's "Britain in Europe" propaganda campaign prepared at the taxpayers' expense.

It may be that Hague privately believes that the UK should leave the EU, but that it is too soon politically to go straight to that stance. That is understandable, insofar as so little has hitherto been done by any individual or group to explain to and prepare the public about the dangers. On the other hand, the longer it takes to rally and channel the surge of Euro-sceptic opinion, the more we become entangled in the Brussels imbroglio. That is why it is so important that the numerous anti-single currency/EMU and the anti-EU groups should coalesce into a more identifiable and high-profile group standing for the UK, democracy and independent nationhood. The urgent task of the anti-EMU/anti-EU groups **is to mount a nation-wide campaign by print, radio and television** to counter and defeat Blair's "Britain in Europe" group and to persuade the people up and down the land that their erstwhile independent country is being shrunken into a provincial unit governed by an unelected unaccountable Orwellian "Animal Farm" of an alien regime in Brussels. The only way to prevent that happening is to recognize the true position and sooner rather than later to make the sea-change by leaving the EU to ensure a life-enhancing future as a renewed independent self-governing nation. However, the first priority is to alert the nation to the **realities**, and to defeat the Government's moves to sink our chances in the single currency/ EMU.

After that, I urge that there are so many advantages and opportunities, outlined in the following passage, for this country to grasp, if it is prepared to throw aside its ghastly bondage, that the ALTERNATIVE is the best, the only, way to be taken by all who love their independence.

The viable, the democratic, the attractive ALTERNATIVE

It cannot be said too often that there is **much more risk, danger and cost for the UK staying in the** EU, with all its suffocating mechanisms, rules and practices, **than leaving it altogether**. After 27 years in the confines of the EU there are likely to be some uncertainties on coming out, during a period of re-adjustment, but they will be as nothing compared with the all too certain disadvantages of staying in, with all its huge costs and burdens. As Lord Beloff said in his comparison of choices, there is no need for such a **"sacrifice"** as the latter course.

And what were the so-called "advantages" to the UK over the 27 years of its Membership? As Lord Lamont, former Chancellor of the Exchequer, said, the advantages of EU Membership are "remarkably elusive", and he really could not think of any. The ostensible benefit is the Single Market, but even the Brussels Commissioner Mario Monti could not say much for it. On the other hand, the **costs and disadvantages of EU Membership** are **colossal and numerous, and ultimately incalculable**. Even before the beginning, the people were misled by Heath and his White Paper about the loss of sovereignty (a conscious untruth since admitted by Heath), and gradually people have realized the true position, and their distrust of Governments has increased. The process of joining the Community distanced us from our old friends in the former Dominions and Colonies and cut short many long-standing trading and other ties in various parts of that world. They who had lived in a close relationship with us and had fought (and many died) in our cause and traded with us for generations had good reason to feel bitterly let down. One of the harsh terms of entry, and a rich prize President Pompidou was amazed at being given so readily, was the British fishery waters, handed over as a "common European resource". This concession has decimated both our entire fishing industry and the fish stocks of the whole zone. But worse is yet to come in this area. Based on Commission Regulation 3760/92, the scheme is for the existing Common Fisheries Policy to be scrapped, and be replaced by the merger of all EU fishing fleets by the year 2003 and a Single Union fleet fishing EU waters under Brussels direction and control. The UK contributions to the EU Budget have amounted to over £100 billion gross and over £30 billion net. Of recent years, the UK gross contribution to the EU Budget is over £9 billion a year, out of which some £6 billion, according to Treasury estimates, goes towards the CAP alone. According to a 1995 National Consumer Council estimate, the CAP costs an average UK family **£20 a week** in higher prices than if food were bought on world markets. I have already mentioned the immense amount of **time** spent by our civil servants, the Government and businesses of all sizes all over the country in understanding, administering and giving effect to Brussels regulations and Directives — time valued in many billions of pounds which should be better spent in running our own affairs. Over all these years we have had to put up with this flood of regulation from the EU and, uniquely in the EU, our civil servants have aggravated this strain by assiduously making the regulations **worse** than on arrival from Brussels. "... much of the regulation is derived not so much from the Community as from the itch of Whitehall to insert its own bureaucratic instincts into the process", as said Douglas (now Lord) Hurd, Foreign Secretary in November 1992.

I believe that the UK is nearing a **watershed** in EU relations. In July 1998 a poll found that 46% of the population wanted us to come OUT of the EU altogether. Over the next twelve months things moved further in that direction and then the Government suffered a serious setback in the Euro-elections. It may well be that the "OUT" percentage has now risen above the halfway mark, to show a majority for leaving the EU. One recalls to mind the words of Brutus about "a tide in the affairs of men" which the British people must take "at the flood"; "omitted, all the voyage of their life is bound in shallows and in miseries".

Why have timid Government and Whitehall been so feebly scared and unsure about our independence? Is the UK so small? So uninfluential? So poor? So inept? So uninventive? Here are some important indicators of the UK's strength and significance:-

(a) We are a considerable nation of almost 60 million population with a long history of democracy and **global** position and influence.

(b) We have a seat on the UN Security Council.

(c) We are a member of G7 group of industrial countries.

(d) We are a member of the World Bank.

(e) We are a member of the International Monetary Fund (IMF).

(f) Our English language is spoken by 1 billion people worldwide and is the main language for the media, international business, science, technology, electronic systems storage, the airways and air traffic control, the seaways and shipping, and increasingly the prime language of Europe.

(g) We are outperforming the EU in trade terms, whilst the EU is underperforming the world.

(h) We have a very big economy with a huge capital market.

(i) Trinity College, Cambridge alone has produced more Nobel prize-winners than the whole of France.

(j) We have vast gross external assets amounting to nearly £2,000 billion, equivalent to the collective GDPs of eleven of the EU Members.

(k) We are the fourth largest world economy.

(l) Our largest trading partner is the USA, bigger than Germany or France.

(m) The USA and Japan are bigger traders with us than Germany and France.

(n) We are global traders, with **over 50%** of our trade with the world **outside the EU**, and our exports **outside the EU** are growing faster than those in the EU.

(o) Our outward direct investment is greater around the world **outside the EU** than in the EU.

(p) According to recent figures (1997), the UK is the third largest recipient of foreign direct investment in the world, after the USA and China.

(q) Inward direct investment into the UK has risen threefold in the period 1987-1997 to £172 billion, whilst the EU's share of global cross-border investment has been falling.

(r) Inward investment had continued to flow since the UK left the ERM in 1992, and has gone on after our Euro-scepticism was widely known abroad.

(s) Foreign direct investment in the UK is **double** that of Germany or France and **four times** that of Italy.

(t) The UK is the preferred location in Europe for US and Japanese investment, and has also attracted large inward investment from Germany and other EU Members.

(u) Funds managed in the UK are some **three times greater** than those in Frankfurt and Paris **combined**.

(v) We have lower tax rates in personal and business taxes than the EU.

(w) We have much lower unemployment than the EU.

(x) We do not have the colossal unfunded pensions liabilities that most of the EU Members have hanging over them.

(y) UK non-wage labour costs are significantly lower than in the majority of EU Members.

(z) The City of London is the greatest financial headquarters of Europe, (unless Brussels attempts to sabotage it). The figures in December 1998 for "invisibles" in International Financial Markets show that: the UK had 19% of the global market for bank lending (France 8%, Germany 7%); the UK had 59% of foreign equity turnover (Germany 2%, France 1%); the UK had 32% of foreign exchange dealing (Germany 5%, France 4%); the UK had 36% of over-the-counter derivatives turnover (France 9%, Germany 7%); and the UK had 66% of the international bond market.

(aa) The UK has nuclear capability and the most highly regarded and imitated military forces in Europe.

Looking at these **27 advantages** which the UK has **in spite of**, and not because of, being in the EU, Blair and his Government cannot be trusted to retain, let alone enhance, them. In fact, the longer this Government are in office, the more these advantages are likely to be reduced or lost altogether, and the more democracy will wither. The **myth** of the advantage of being in the EU really is the

Adolf Hitler "great lie" referred to in his *Mein Kampf* and quoted earlier.

I will stress, though it should be plain, that whether or not the UK leaves the EU, we will, as we have done for hundreds of years, go on trading with all the other EU Members, and with Norway, Switzerland and all the other countries of Europe. Here are **a number of gains, advantages and freedoms we would achieve on the UK LEAVING the EU**:

(i) We would have cheaper food, being free from the CAP burdens.

(ii) We would be able to rebuild our fishing industry and our fishing fleet, and re-establish our territorial waters, free from the CFP.

(iii) Our Government, our Parliament and our Supreme Court would all operate again, free from the restrictive predominance and interference of the EU institutions and the European Court of Human Rights.

(iv) We would escape from the suffocating burden of the EU acquis communautaire with its 23,000 regulations.

(v) We would be free from the threat or reality of the single currency/EMU straitjacket and the handing over of our reserves of £28 billion.

(vi) We would no longer have to pay EU Budget contributions which are certain to increase, thus saving many billions of pounds for home investment.

(vii) We would enhance our position as a **global** free trader with all the countries of the world, unconfined by protective tariffs of "Fortress Europe".

(viii) The Central and Eastern European Countries (CEECs) wold be glad to increase trade with the UK, without the EU import restrictions. **Free trade is the "great danger" ... "precisely what we have been trying to avoid for the past 25 years"**, according to former Commissioner Yves-Thibault de Silguy in 1996.

(ix) We would avoid punitive EU harmonizing taxes which would restrict or decimate our trading and investment activities.

(x)   Our leaders could spend their time running our own country, instead of obeying every command from Brussels, and being regarded in Brussels and Strasbourg as the "awkward squad" always resisting, arguing, compromising and losing, and coming home pretending they had done so well.

(xi)   Similarly, our civil servants could again work wholly on UK business, not as at present spending two-thirds of their time obeying and enforcing Brussels diktats.

(xii)   We should work hard to re-establish and improve our former links and friendships with those free-trading independent countries who were Dominions and Colonies all over the world, and do our best to erase their old feelings of betrayal at Heath's shameful disloyalty in 1972.

(xiii)   We should seek increased trade with the USA and the other countries of the North Atlantic Free Trade Area (NAFTA), and also with the countries of MERCOSUR (the South American free trade association), as well as with China, Japan and the other countries of Asia.

(xiv)   We should continue to play our part in the UN Security Council, the G7 group of industrial countries, the World Bank, and the IMF, without our position in any of them being threatened by encroachment or usurpation by the EU.

(xv)   The City of London could continue, and develop further, as the prime European centre of banking, investment, dealing and fund management in all their forms, without hindrance or damage from Brussels in the way of taxation or other legislation.

(xvi)   We would be free to set our own interest rates, without looking over our shoulder at the requirements of the new ERM.

(xvii)   We could sweep away thousands of harmful and restrictive regulations emanating from or caused by the Brussels machine, revitalize damaged businesses, and help back to life businesses bankrupted by those regulations.

(xviii)   We would be free from any future EU threat to expropriate our oil and gas rights, stocks and reserves as "common European resources".

(xix)   We would not be subjected to any EU multi-billion pound transport network schemes, including, for instance, the requirement to change our entire road systems for driving on the righthand side of the road.

These are some of the most obvious gains and freedoms for the UK on **leaving the EU**. If one looks through Maastricht and Amsterdam, there are many more burdensome and costly provisions which could and should be avoided by coming OUT of the EU, and there will be again many more such provisions in the next and subsequent Treaties leading to a Federal Union.

I have outlined **27 advantages** that the UK has as a major nation with **global** interests whose position would be **enhanced** by leaving the EU. I have also indicated **19 gains and freedoms** which would be available and would enormously benefit the UK on leaving the EU. Many more advantages and gains could be identified, given more time and space, but I believe that what is here is sufficient **to make the case for the UK LEAVING the EU**, though maintaining a close, friendly and easier relationship with all the Member States.

"The Parliament and Commission are allies *against* the Member States. Together we have to prevent the Member States from *taking back* power". This revealing comment was made by a German MEP on Radio 4 on 20th July 1999. The words in italics each stress a point: the first shows the common stance of the EU institutions in their continuous pressure against the Member States for hegemony in the Community, their objective being to have the Commission as the Executive Government of the Federal Union of Europe; the second clearly acknowledges that sovereignty has already largely been surrendered by the Member States. Russian and Eastern European Communism has ended in failure, and its first cousin, the centralized Socialist bureaucracy of the EU, is also rusty and outdated. The EU is yesterday's system, unsuitable for today and tomorrow, unstably based on French-style dirigiste protectionism and on proportional representation of the German model. This inward-looking, sclerotic, factious creature is not what is needed for a healthy future for the UK, nor for global development and amity. Blair and his Government are gradually by stealth ("slowly and unconsciously") moving our country into that dire condition. In *Eastern Approaches* Sir Fitzroy Maclean quoted a German diplomat's remark about Adolf Hitler after the Munich appeasement: "... he does not understand your mentality. He does not realize that, whatever line your Government may take, there is a limit beyond which you, as a nation, will not be prepared to let him go". I truly hope that the national spirit has survived in sufficient strength over the intervening 60 years for this view still to hold good. I believe that it has, but it needs reawakening, and the population must be alerted and informed before it is too late. **Let our historic island people resoundingly reject defeatism and herald a triumphant resurgence in self-belief, pride and independence.**

ENVOI

In the autumn of 2000, with the Nice Summit and Treaty almost upon us, it is worth briefly touching on a few recent and forthcoming matters:

- **Austria**: Diplomatic sanctions against Austria, set in place largely by France and Germany, and with no legitamacy under the Treaties, were lifted by the EU in September 2000. How far this was done to assist the Danish Referendum on the Single Currency towards a Yes decision, is not known.

- **The Danish Referendum**: On 28th September 2000 the Danish people spoke a firm No to joining the Single Currency and to the loss of national control over their economic and monetary issues, and to the wider political implications which would otherwise have ensued. This verdict, in the face of the strong opposition of their Government and their whole media and Establishment, is enormously to the credit of the Danish people and their spirit of independence.

- **The euro**: The sorry tale of its fall has continued, despite substantial monetary intervention by the ECB and some Member State Governments. Intervention seldom works, and it is often merely pouring good money after bad. Because of lack of credibility in the euro, in the 20 months to September 2000 there was a serious flight of capital from Member States amounting to an outflow of some £200 billion. In September 2000 polls in the UK showed that those against the Single currency in the political parties amounted to: 58% Labour, 66% Liberal Democrats and 84% Conservatives.

- **Inward Investment**: A recent Report from UNCTAD shows that the UK is still the most popular place for inward investment, which rose again in 1999 in spite of our not being in the Single Currency.

- **The London Stock Exchange merger**: The LSE merger with the Deutsche Börse of Frankfurt was scrapped, after a take-over bid supervened from the Swedish OM Group. It was incomprehensible that the LSE, with many times more daily foreign exchange and other dealing business than the small Frankfurt Exchange, was prepared to merge and become a subordinate partner. Was this failed project the outcome of the LSE's ineptitude and lack of business acumen, or was it part of a plan to manoeuvre the UK towards the Single Currency and entangle the LSE in continental business practises, including the dangers of tax harmonization and the damaging witholding tax?

- **The EU Commission's new anti-fraud office, OLAF**: It was reported in August 2000 that OLAF is a failure, and that fraud and corruption are a continuing substantial drain on EU Budget funds. It is ironic, but typical of the Commission, that the overlord of OLAF is the EU Budget Commissioner.

- **United Europe:** At their October 2000 meeting in Dresden, Chancellor Schroder and President Chirac agreed to use Germany's federal State as a model for a United Europe.

- **The Treaty of Nice**: The Draft Treaty is not readily available to the UK general public, but, as we know, the broad thrust will be ever onwards towards integration and ultimate Union. More specifically, the Charter of Fundamental Rights is on the agenda. It was drafted by a Convention chaired by former President Herzog of Germany, who was reported years ago as saying "Our aim is the end of the nation state". Seen by a number of EU leaders as the cornerstone of a future EU Constitution, it contains some 54 rights, some of which are reportedly new, though the Charter's defenders say that none are new and all are only declaratory. The UK

Government agreed to it at the beginning of October 2000, before the Biarritz Summit in that month, and it maintains that it is not legally binding. However, the EU Commission say that the Charter is a major milestone for the EU as a political force. And Antonio Vitorino, the EU Justice and Home Affairs Commissioner, said that the European Court of Justice will use the Charter as a reference text in reaching decisions, even if it were purely a declamatory document. In addition, the Commission and certain Member States want to see the Charter included in the Treaty itself.

The Treaty will also seek to remove the veto in a further number of areas. And the Commission with support from the EU Parliament are pressing for a fully fledged EU Foreign Service. Further developments are also being urged for a Common Defence Policy and in the field of EU Criminal law and Courts systems. And so on.

It should be realized, and surely is, that the EU saga continues like an everflowing stream as developments follow one upon the other, and the Acquis increases its already gigantic size. In a few weeks and months, existing issues will have progressed and new ones will have arisen, but they will be beyond the province of this book.

FURTHER LIST OF READING AND REFERENCE

1. "Treaty of Amsterdam", (590 pages) copy from Foreign & Commonwealth Office, November 1997.

2. "The Treaty of Amsterdam in Perspective - Consolidated Treaty of European Union", (350 pages), British Management Data Foundation, January 1998.

3. "Britain: A Global Future", Bill Jamieson, March 1997.

4. "Britain: Free to Choose", Bill Jamieson, Global Britain Research Group, 1998.

5. "A Coming Home or Poisoned Chalice?" Szamuely and Jamieson, Centre for Research into Post-Communist Economics, March 1998.

6. "Britain and European Union - Dialogue of the Deaf", Lord Beloff 1996.

7. "A Price not worth paying - the economic cost of EMU", Burkitt, Baimbridge & Whyman, Campaign for an Independent Britain, July 1996.

8. "The Euro: Bad for Britain", European Research Group, December 1998.

9. "The Euro: Bad for Business", European Research Group, December 1998.

10. "Business for Sterling. The Case for Keeping the Pound", Business for Sterling, 1998.

11. "Report on the First Congress for Democracy", December 1998, The European Research Group.

12. "The UK and the Euro - better out than in?" Institute of Directors 1999.

13. "The Tainted Source", John Laughland, 1998.

14. "A business view of EMU", a Survey of Business Opinion, Nelson & Pollard Publishing, November 1996.

15. "UK Membership of the Single Currency", H.M. Treasury, October 1997.

16. "The pros and cons of EMU", David Currie, H.M. Treasury, July 1997.

17. Financial Times Guide to EMU, 1998.

18. "Britain in Europe - the Next Phase", Stratagems Publishing, 1998.

19. "Britain and Europe: Choices for Change", Jamieson & Minford, 1999.

20. "Better Off Out?", Hindley & Howe, IEA, 1998.

21. "British Influence and the euro", Sir John Coles, New Europe, 1999.

22. "Adapting the Institutions to make a success of Enlargement". The EU Commission Opinion, 26 January 2000.

23. "IGC: Reform for Enlargement Government", White Paper, Command 4595, February 2000.

24. "Better Off Out", Lord Pearson of Rannoch, July 2000.

25. "Separate Ways" Peter (Lord) Shore, Duckworth, 2000.

26. "Statement of General Principles", New Europe.

27. "Continent Cut Off? The macroeconomic impact of British withdrawal from the EU", Pain & Young, NIESR, 2000.

28. "EU Membership: What's the Bottom Line?", Graeme Leach, IoD Policy Paper, 2000.

29. "The UK and the Euro - better out than in?", Graeme Leach, IoD Research Paper 1999.

30. "A Competitive Britain in a competitive Europe", Ruth Lea, IoD, 1999.

31. "UK Membership of the Euro", Ruth Lea, IoD Survey.

32. "The Euro: Bad for Trade Unions", Doug Nicholls, General Secretary of CYWU, 1999.

33. "EMU - Not very sensible", Simon Wolfson.

34. "eurofacts", fortnightly papers, Global Britain.

35. "Blowing the Whistle", Paul van Buitenen, Politicos.

36. "Independence", Journal and newsletters of the CIB.

37. "Newsletters", from New Europe.

38. "Vachers European Companion", Quarterly, Vacher, Dod Publishing.